Artificial Intelligence:
To Trust Or Not To Trust,
That Is The Question

-

Preface

Artificial intelligence is certainly a hot topic these days, but have you ever wondered: What is it? What does it do? How does it work? Is it a good thing or a bad thing? Should we trust it? What role is it already playing in our lives? What role might it play in the future? Should we be worried about it? Is it a threat to our livelihood, our jobs, our privacy, even our existence?

If you have, then this book is for you. The author attempts to address these questions and more in a way that is both informative and accessible to non-experts. Evidence and examples from both sides of the debate are presented, together with suggestions for some practical steps that need to be taken sooner rather than later. After reading this book you will hopefully know more about Artificial Intelligence than you did – but will you feel more or less comfortable with AI?

"Artificial intelligence is one of the most profound things we're working on as humanity. It is more profound than fire or electricity."
- Sundar Pichai, 2020

About The Author

Paul Hind holds an Honours Degree in Psychology, a Masters Distinction in Computing and is currently doing PhD research in Human/Artificial Intelligence interactions and relations.

The author would like to thank Sandra Scrafton, BA (Hons), for her tireless work and unfailing attention to detail during the proof reading of this book.

Chapters

CH1: AI: History

"The Navy revealed the embryo of an electronic computer today that it expects will be able to walk, talk, see, write, reproduce itself, and be conscious of its existence" - New York Times 1958

"Machines will be capable, within twenty years, of doing any work that a man can do" - Herbert Simon, American political scientist, 1960

The idea of Artificial Intelligence can be traced back to 1942 when Isaac Asimov, an American science fiction writer, first published a story called 'Runaround'. The plot of this and several of Asimov's later works, revolved around 'The Three Laws of Robotics':

1) A robot may not injure a human beingor, through inaction, allow a human being to come to harm.
2) A robot must obey the orders given to it by human beings, except where such orders would conflict with the First Law.
3) A robot must protect its own existence, so long as such protection does not conflict with the First or Second Laws.

As well as providing fascination and entertainment to his readers, Asimov inspired generations of scientists in the field of robotics, Artificial Intelligence (AI) and computer science, including the American cognitive scientist Marvin Minsky (who later co-founded the MIT AI laboratory and was an advisor to Stanley Kubrick for his film 2001: A Space Odyssey).

It was around the same time, during the Second World War, that an English mathematician named Alan Turing developed, for the British Government, a machine to decipher the Enigma code being used by the German army. The machine, which was over six feet tall and about the same in width, with a weight of about one ton, was called 'The Bombe' and is considered by many to be the first working electro-mechanical computer.

In 1950, Turing published an article with the title 'Computing Machinery and Intelligence', in which he described, not only the process for creating intelligent machines, but also a suggestion for how they might be tested. He proposed that, if a human were to interact with a machine and not be able to distinguish it from another human, then that machine should be considered 'intelligent'. The 'Turing Test' became a benchmark for identifying Artificial Intelligence.

In 1954 Joseph Engelberger, the 'Father of Robotics' and a huge fan of Isaac Asimov, developed 'Unimate', a robotic arm he based on designs by American inventor George Devol. He gained approval for his robots by employing them on tasks normally regarded as dangerous for humans, with the first prototype being installed on General Motors' diecasting production line in 1959.

At a summer conference held at Dartmouth University in 1956 the 'Logic Theorist' was presented. As a program that could prove theorems in symbolic logic from Whitehead and Russell's Principia Mathematica (a three-volume work on the foundations of mathematics), it is generally considered the first working program that simulated some aspects of human problem-solving abilities.

Nobel Prize winner Herbert Simon, together with colleagues from the RAND Corporation (an American non-profit global policy think-tank created in 1948 to offer research and analysis to the United States Armed Forces), developed the 'General Problem Solver' program in 1959, to solve certain types of simple puzzles, like the Towers of Hanoi (a mathematical puzzle consisting of three rods and a number of disks of various diameters, which can slide onto any rod. The puzzle begins with the disks stacked on one rod in order of decreasing size, the smallest at the top. The objective of the puzzle is to move the entire stack to the last rod, whilst obeying certain rules).

Unfortunately, the General Problem Solver (GPS) could not solve any real-world problems because progress was easily lost in the combinatorial explosion (the rapid growth of the complexity of a problem owing to how it is affected by the input, constraints and bounds of the problem). The GPS paradigm did, however, eventually evolve into the Soar architecture (both a theory of what cognition is and a computational implementation of that theory), for Artificial Intelligence.

One of the first programs that attempted to pass the Turing Test was created by Joseph Weizenbaum at the MIT Artificial Intelligence Laboratory in 1966. It was a natural language processing tool called ELIZA, which used pattern matching and substitution methodologies designed to give an illusion of understanding. ELIZA was able to process user inputs and engage by following the directions of a script. Despite many users' opinions to the contrary, ELIZA could not converse with true understanding. However, the source-code she used is of great historical interest as it demonstrates, not only the specificity of programming languages and techniques at that time, but also the beginning of software layering and abstraction as a means of achieving sophisticated software programming.

The late 1960s saw the advent of the first general-purpose robot that was able to reason about its own actions. Developed at the Artificial Intelligence Centre of Stanford Research Institute, Shakey the robot could analyse commands given to it and break them down into basic tasks, thereby becoming the first project that melded logical reasoning and physical action.

These and other exciting developments encouraged substantial funding for AI research, culminating in Marvin Minsky's interview with Life Magazine in 1970 when he proposed that, in less than eight years, a machine would exist with similar general intelligence to a human.

Unfortunately, just three years later, high levels of spending began attracting criticism from the U.S. Congress. Meanwhile, largely because of a report published by the mathematician James Lighthill, in which he insisted that machines would always be limited to playing simple rule-based games and could never be capable of common-sense reasoning, the British Government limited AI research to just three universities (Edinburgh, Sussex and Essex), so beginning what has been termed 'The AI Winter'.

An upturn in enthusiasm came in the 1980s when Japan made the decision to invest heavily in a new generation of computing systems with ambitious AI capabilities at its core. The US was forced to respond with its 'Strategic Computing Initiative', pouring large sums of money into general AI generation projects. Sadly, by the end of the decade, all hopes were once more dashed by a failure to produce the results that had been dreamed of.

Expert Systems:

Early systems like ELIZA and the General Problem Solver relied on collections of rules which made them, what might be termed, Expert Systems. The assumption behind such systems is that human intelligence can be formalised and reconstructed as a series of 'if-then' statements in a top-down approach. In 1997 IBM's Deep Blue chess playing program used just such an approach, processing possible moves at the rate of 200 million per second and looking 20 moves ahead via a method called 'tree searching', to beat Gary Kasparov, the then world champion.

Unfortunately, Expert Systems are not always so successful in other areas. Facial recognition, for example, is a real problem for them, since success here requires a system that can interpret external data, learn from it and then use that knowledge to achieve particular goals through flexible adaptation.The fundamental weakness of Expert Systems is that, when human experts write the rules, they rely on subconscious knowledge or 'common sense' which is not part of the system's programming.

Neural Network Systems:

Attempts to achieve true AI through statistical systems go back to the 1940s when the Canadian psychologist Donald Hebb developed and gave his name to Hebbian Learning, a theory of learning that seeks to replicate the processes that occur in and between neurons in the human brain. This research on Neural Networks hit a wall in 1969 when Marvin Minsky and Seymour Papert proved that the computers of the time had nowhere near the processing power necessary to support such networks.

The Neural Network approaches of the 1980s and 1990s represented a new approach to Artificial Intelligence that teaches computers to process data in a way that is inspired by the human brain. It is a type of Machine Learning process, called Deep Learning, that uses interconnected nodes or neurons in a layered structure that resembles the human brain. It worked well in certain areas but lacked the adaptability to tackle more complex problems in a way that might earn it the right to be considered general intelligence.

Machine Learning:

During the 1990s and into the 2000s algorithms began to be developed that could create predictive models from data fed to them. This Machine Learning approach found its origins not in psychology or neuroscience but in statistics, with the aim of performing specific tasks rather than capturing general intelligence. Indeed, the developers of these systems were keen to separate themselves and their methods from the generally discredited field of AI.

A Return to Neural Networks:

By 2010 things had changed quite dramatically with the advent of much faster parallel computing chips (Moore's Law – an observation rather than a law of physics – pointed out that the quantity of transistors that could be included in one integrated circuit doubles every two years), alongside the availability of unprecedented amounts of data available from the Web and vastly improved training methods developed by a growing community of specialist researchers using clusters of graphics processing units (GPUs). The term 'AI' began to appear everywhere, as Deep Neural Networks spawned major advances that reignited enthusiasm for general or human-level Artificial Intelligence.

By this point, Google's autonomous driving cars had logged over 140,000 miles on the road, leading the company to boast that it had the ability to cut traffic deaths by half.

This was also the year when IBM, through its DeepQA project, presented 'Watson', a computer system capable of answering questions posed in natural language. It was able to do this by combining over one hundred techniques, analysing natural language, identifying sources, generating hypotheses, then finding and rating evidence to merge and rank those hypotheses. In 2011 Watson competed on a TV quiz show called Jeopardy and won against two champion players, to claim a prize of one million dollars.

Further evidence of the power of these Neural Network systems to effectively carry out tasks previously considered too complex for any machine to master was provided in 2012 by an image recognition system called AlexNet, which effectively halved error rates of rival systems.

In 2015 these Deep or Artificial Neural Networks took centre stage in the form of a Deep Learning program developed by Google, designed to play a board game far more sophisticated than chess called Go (eg. chess begins with 20 possible moves, whereas Go starts with 361). AlphaGo works by having two Neural Networks. The first one, referred to as the "policy network", selects the next move to play. The other Neural Network is referred to as the "value network", and it predicts the winner of the game. During training AlphaGo was introduced to a number of amateur games to help develop an understandable image of what reasonable human play looked like. It then played against different versions of itself thousands of times to learn from its mistakes. Using Reinforcement Learning, AlphaGo improved and became much stronger at learning and decision-making tasks. Even though the search that it uses is initially based on human-like preferences, AlphaGo can override the bias if it discovers a move that leads to a better outcome.

The AlphaGo program was able to first beat the European champion Fan Hull five games to zero before going on to triumph against the world champion Lee Sedol by four games to one. A new version of the program has recently been presented by Google DeepMind CEO Demis Hassabis that has mastered both chess and shogi.

In that same year Mark Zuckerberg, Facebook's CEO said, "One of our goals for the next five to ten years is to basically get better than human-level at all the primary human senses: vision, hearing, language and general cognition."

Since then, artificial Neural Networks and Deep Learning have become the basis for most of the applications commonly referred to as AI, including the speech recognition algorithms of smart speakers, machine translation, protein folding, self-driving cars and Facebook's image recognition algorithms.

In 2020 a not-for-profit organisation called OpenAI appeared to have produced an AI system that could write and speak like a person about a multitude of topics. Called Generative Pre-trained Transformer 3 (GPT-3), it is a Neural Network that has been trained on billions of website articles and can answer questions on a broad range of subjects. However, after closer scrutiny, it was found that some of the system's output was actually nonsense.

Later that same year, however, came a still more striking example of the possible potential of Artificial Intelligence when AlphaFold 2, an attention-based network system developed by Google, produced a result that many said would, if produced by a human, be worthy of a Nobel Prize for Chemistry. The 3D structure of a protein is a vitally important element, the understanding of which can have a dramatic impact on understanding of diseases and development of medicines. Until now, the gold standard for modelling proteins has been crystallography, a process that requires months to produce results. The developers found that AlphaFold 2 could reduce that processing time to mere hours, representing a landmark breakthrough for medical science.

Despite its success, however, Deep Learning can still be susceptible to errors when dealing with situations that do not entirely match with its training data. The problem is something that experts call 'Shortcut Learning', which occurs when the system produces correct answers but for the wrong reasons. "Why does the reasoning matter, so long as the answer is right?" you may wonder. It matters because it demonstrates that the machine is not learning the abstract concepts we want it to and consequently cannot generalise what it has learned to new problems. These systems are also vulnerable to the effects of 'adversarial perturbations': changes in the input that humans either cannot detect or consider of no importance, but which cause the system to make errors.

Modern Neural Networks are extremely complicated systems with enormous ranges of parameters, which result in decision-making mechanisms that to humans may appear completely opaque, a situation commonly referred to as 'black box decision making'. Despite huge amounts of research, so far these problems remain and have generated a debate in the AI community as to whether true understanding of the 'humankind' can ever be achieved by adding yet more network layers and more training data, or whether something far more fundamental is being missed.

In the mean-time work goes on with research into new Deep Learning systems such as Transformer Architectures which use Self-Supervised Learning, where Machine Learning algorithms determine how to best combine the predictions of other Machine Learning algorithms and Deep Reinforcement Learning where the system decides to take actions based on gaining certain rewards.

The history of Artificial Intelligence is, therefore, not just the history of mechanical attempts to replicate or replace some static notion of human intelligence, but also a changing account of how we think about intelligence itself.

The question has now become, not whether AI will play a role in governments, businesses and individual private lives, but rather how might AI and humans comfortably coexist. Which, in turn, means addressing the question of which decisions should be made by AI, which by humans alone and which by a collaboration of the two.

CH2: AI: A Definition

"AI is human-like intelligence exhibited by machines" - Yves De Smet, 2017

"AI is a system that simulates human intellectual functioning. In doing so, it allows a rational computation of datasets to come up with an output in a form or shape desired by the programmer" - Science Direct, 2021

When we say or hear the phrase "Artificial Intelligence" (or "AI") various things can come to mind, from images of robot armies trying to extinguish humanity to less intimidating images of Alexa asking someone trivia questions.

Most people are not very familiar with the concept of Artificial Intelligence (AI). As an illustration, when, in 2017, 1,500 senior business leaders in the United States were asked about AI, only 17 percent said they were familiar with it. A number of them were not sure what it was or how it would affect their particular companies. They understood there was considerable potential for altering business processes, but were not clear how AI could be deployed within their own organizations.

There is no general legal definition for what constitutes AI outside of a specific application, such as in the context of autonomous automobiles or electronic agents trading in the markets, but the applications of AI are expanding to a point where it will be impractical to define it for every application.

We have AI in our cars, in our mobile phones, and in our video games. We have AI in medicine, in military applications and in government agencies. It's getting harder to find an aspect of our daily lives that doesn't purport to have some kind of interaction with AI. We are relinquishing more of the personal and professional decision-making process to vestiges of evolving notions of AI. Not only are we starting to defer to AI for the decision-making process, we are subtly transferring the ultimate responsibility for the decisions and the consequences of those decisions, to AI. The public's acceptance and reliance on various aspects of AI is becoming normalized. One major problem with this scenario is that, as a society, we are unclear about what constitutes AI. Our social position on AI is: we may not be able to define it concisely or correctly, but we all know it when we see it, right? Clearly the integral part that AI has in our society makes this position untenable and we can and should do better with our definition.

With the promise of efficiency and money, companies have begun pursuing Artificial Intelligence and investing copious amounts of money into its development. Governments and legislatures have certainly taken note, and some states have attempted to outline regulations for Artificial Intelligence. Without definitions, or at the very least a clear understanding of the concept, many resources will be wasted on litigation and inept policy making.

Neither scientists, programmers, philosophers or lawyers have a clear understanding of what AI is. Attempting to define AI is nothing new, but what is different now is the necessity of a definition, and specifically a legal definition.

So why is it so difficult to produce a meaningful definition of AI? Broadly speaking, there are three reasons:

1. It is already difficult to define what human intelligence is and, hence, applying this fuzzy concept to machines is a complicated endeavour.
2. Once we grow used to a machine performing a complex task, we stop considering the ability to do this task a sign of intelligence. This is generally referred to as the 'AI effect' and it makes the definition of AI a moving target in the sense that it always seems to be out of reach.
3. AI has different evolutionary stages: from narrow to general to super intelligence and can be classified into analytical, human-inspired, and humanized AI, depending on its cognitive, emotional, and social competences. It is easy to mix up those

different stages and types, leading to confusion over the term itself.

The hang-up in defining AI is, in large part, because of the ambiguity of "intelligence". We recognize intelligence in ourselves, so we link our understanding of intelligence to human characteristics. One understanding of intelligence is tied to the ability to perform intellectual tasks. However, as technology advances, so too do the tasks computers can accomplish. As machines accomplish more tasks, we tend not to consider them as reaching intelligence, but instead we move the threshold of intelligence farther away and then treat that specific task as unindicative of intelligence. What counts as intelligence is a moving target in the history of Artificial Intelligence.

To answer the question of whether something has intelligence, there needs to be some form of measurement. The Turing test has withstood the advancement of technology because it forces the computer to imitate human behaviour, giving it a strong anthropocentric bias. For instance, what we consider simple questions-like, "what is your oldest memory?" or "what was your most painful moment?" quickly expose that one is speaking to a machine rather than another human being.

The most distinct characteristic of intelligence is autonomy. Autonomy is a condition of thinking which allows for the attribution of thinking or intelligence to children and animals, but not machines, as machines just do as they are told. However, as machines are becoming more advanced, AI systems are beginning to exhibit and exercise autonomy - making decisions free from outside input. This is by design, as Machine Learning systems need to be free from human input, otherwise they simply could not learn or function as intended. To be clear, there was human input in the form of the initial programming, but the purpose of the system is to learn and to provide unprogrammed outputs.

A clear, concise definition or presentation of intelligence for the laymen or the public at large is a tall order. Let's have a look at some recent attempts:

"Intelligence is the efficiency with which you acquire new skills at tasks you didn't previously prepare for."

"Intelligence is not skill itself; it's not what you can do; it's how well and how efficiently you can learn new things."

"Intelligence refers to a system's ability to interpret external data correctly, to learn from such data, and to use those learnings to achieve specific goals and tasks through flexible adaptation."

We in the AI community have a solemn obligation to define what we mean by Artificial Intelligence, its limits, its applicable scope, failure rates, risks, potential benefits and costs. We must find a way to clearly and effectively educate and inform the public about this technology. In doing so we need to address some of the misconceptions that complicate our task. Over-optimism among the public, the media, and even experts can arise from several fallacies in how we talk about AI and in our intuitions about the nature of intelligence. Understanding these fallacies and their subtle influences can point to directions for creating more robust, trustworthy, and perhaps actually intelligent AI systems:

- **Fallacy 1: Narrow intelligence is on a continuum with general intelligence:**
  If people see a machine do something amazing, albeit in a narrow area, they often assume the field is that much further along toward general AI. The philosopher Hubert Dreyfus (using a term coined by Yehoshua Bar-Hillel) called this a "first-step fallacy." As Dreyfus characterized it, "The first-step fallacy is the claim that, ever since our first work on computer intelligence we have been inching along a continuum at the end of which is AI, so that any improvement in our programs, no matter how trivial, counts as progress." Dreyfus quotes an analogy made by his brother, the engineer Stuart Dreyfus: "It was like claiming that the first monkey that climbed a tree was making progress towards landing on the moon". Like many AI experts before and after him, Dreyfus

noted that the "unexpected obstacle" in the assumed continuum of AI progress has always been the problem of common sense.

- **Fallacy 2: Easy things are easy and hard things are hard:**
The things that we humans do without much thought—looking out on the world and making sense of what we see; carrying on a conversation; walking down a crowded street without bumping into anyone - turn out to be the hardest challenges for machines. Conversely, it's often easier to get machines to do things that are very hard for humans; for example, solving complex mathematical problems, mastering games like chess and Go, and translating sentences into hundreds of languages have all turned out to be relatively easier for machines.

  Researchers at Google DeepMind, in talking about AlphaGo's triumph, described the game of Go as one of "the most challenging of domains". Challenging for whom? For humans, perhaps, but as psychologist Gary Marcus pointed out, there are domains, including games, that, while easy for humans, are much more challenging than Go for AI systems. One example is charades, which requires acting skills, linguistic skills, and theory of mind: abilities that are far beyond anything AI can accomplish today.

  Hans Moravec explains the paradox this way: "Encoded in the large, highly evolved sensory and motor portions of the human brain is a billion years of experience about the nature of the world and how to survive in it. The deliberate process we call reasoning is, I believe, the thinnest veneer of human thought, effective only because it is supported by this much older and much more powerful, though usually unconscious, sensorimotor knowledge".

- **Fallacy 3: The lure of wishful mnemonics:**
Work on AI is replete with wishful mnemonics - terms associated with human intelligence that are used to describe the behaviour

and evaluation of AI programs. Neural networks are loosely inspired by the brain, but with vast differences. Machine learning or Deep Learning methods do not really resemble learning in humans (or in non-human animals). Indeed, if a machine has learned something in the human sense of learn, we would expect that it would be able use what it has learned in different contexts. However, it turns out that this is often not the case. In Machine Learning there is an entire subfield called transfer learning that focuses on the still-open problem of how to enable machines to transfer what they have learned to new situations, an ability that is fundamental to human learning.

IBM scientists know that Watson doesn't read or understand in the way humans do; DeepMind scientists know that AlphaGo has no goals or thoughts in the way humans do, and no human-like conceptions of a "game" or of "winning." However, such shorthand can be misleading to the public trying to understand these results (and to the media reporting on them) and can also unconsciously shape the way even AI experts think about their systems and how closely these systems resemble human intelligence.

The research community also uses wishful mnemonics in naming AI evaluation benchmarks after the skills we hope they test. For example, here are some of the most widely cited current benchmarks in the subarea of AI called "Natural Language Processing" (NLP):
* the "Stanford Question Answering Dataset"
* the "RACE Reading Comprehension Dataset"
* the "General Language Understanding Evaluation"

In all of these benchmarks, the performance of the best machines has already exceeded that measured for humans (typically Amazon Mechanical Turk workers). This has led to headlines such as "New AI model exceeds human performance at question answering"; "Computers are getting better than humans at reading"; and "Microsoft's AI model has outperformed humans in natural-language understanding".

Given the names of these benchmark evaluations, it's not surprising that people would draw such conclusions. The problem is, these benchmarks don't actually measure general abilities for question-answering, reading comprehension, or natural-language understanding. The benchmarks test only very limited versions of these abilities; moreover, many of these benchmarks allow machines to learn shortcuts, as described above - statistical correlations that machines can exploit to achieve high performance on the test without learning the actual skill being tested. While machines can outperform humans on these particular benchmarks, AI systems are still far from matching the more general human abilities we associate with the benchmarks' names.

- **Fallacy 4: Intelligence is all in the brain:**
  The idea that intelligence is something that can be separated from the body, whether as a non-physical substance or as wholly encapsulated in the brain, has a long history in philosophy and cognitive science. The so-called "information-processing model of mind" arose in psychology in the mid-twentieth century. This model views the mind as a kind of computer, which inputs, stores, processes, and outputs information. The body does not play much of a role except in the input (perception) and output (behaviour) stages. Under this view, cognition takes place wholly in the brain, and is, in theory, separable from the rest of the body. An extreme corollary of this view is that, in the future, we will be able to "upload" our brains—and thus our cognition and consciousness— to computers.

The assumption that intelligence can in principle be "disembodied" is implicit in almost all work on AI throughout its history. Grounded in the post-war traditions of systems engineering and cybernetics and drawing from the longer history of mathematical logic and philosophy aimed at formal descriptions of human thinking, it has generally been held that cognitive faculties could be abstracted from the supporting physical operations of the brain. Thus, the former could, in principle, be reproduced in different material substrata, so long as the formal rules could be executed there.

Herbert Simon and Allen Newell influentially proposed, more specifically, that human minds and modern digital computers were 'species of the same genus,' namely symbolic information processing systems: both take symbolic information as input, manipulate it according to a set of formal rules, and in so doing solve problems, formulate judgments, and make decisions.

Today's deep Neural Networks are akin to the proverbial brain-in-a-vat: passively taking in data from the world and outputting instructions for behaviour without actively interacting in the world with any kind of body. Of course, robots and autonomous vehicles are different in that they have a physical presence in the world but, to date, the kinds of physical interactions they have, and the feedback to their "intelligence" is quite limited.

The assumption that intelligence is all in the brain has led to speculation that, to achieve human-level AI, we simply need to scale up machines to match the brain's "computing capacity" and then develop the appropriate "software" for this brain-matching "hardware.

A growing cadre of researchers, however, is questioning the basis of the "all in the brain" information processing model for understanding intelligence and for creating AI. Several cognitive scientists have argued for decades in favour of the centrality of the body in all cognitive activities. Psychologist Rebecca Fincher-Kiefer characterizes the embodied cognition paradigm this way: "Embodied cognition means that the representation of conceptual knowledge is dependent on the body: it is multimodal..., not amodal, symbolic, or abstract. This theory suggests that our thoughts are grounded, or inextricably associated with, perception, action, and emotion, and that our brain and body work together to create cognition". Examples of this include painting, dancing and performing tai chi.

Research in neuroscience suggests, for example, that the neural structures controlling cognition are richly linked to those controlling sensory and motor systems, and that abstract thinking exploits body-based neural "maps". As neuroscientist Don Tucker noted, "There are no brain parts for disembodied cognition". Results from cognitive psychology and linguistics indicate that many, if not all, of our abstract concepts are grounded in physical, body-based internal models.

Related to the theory of embodied cognition is the idea that the emotions and the "irrational" biases that exist in our deeply social lives - typically thought of as separate from intelligence, or as getting in the way of rationality - are actually key to what makes intelligence possible.

AI is often thought of as aiming at a kind of "pure intelligence," one that is independent of emotions, irrationality, and constraints of the body such as the need to eat and sleep. This assumption of the possibility of a purely rational intelligence can lead to lurid predictions about the risks we will face from future "super intelligent" machines.

Stuart Russell worries about the possible outcomes of employing such a super intelligence to solve humanity's problems: "What if a super intelligent climate control system, given the job of restoring carbon dioxide concentrations to preindustrial levels, believes the solution is to reduce the human population to zero? If we insert the wrong objective into the machine and it is more intelligent than us, we lose".

The thought experiments proposed by Bostrom and Russell seem to assume that an AI system could be "super intelligent" without any basic humanlike common sense, while seamlessly preserving the speed, precision and programmability of a computer. But these speculations about superhuman AI are plagued by flawed intuitions about the nature of intelligence. Nothing in our knowledge of psychology or neuroscience supports the possibility that "pure rationality" is separable from the emotions and cultural biases that shape our cognition and our objectives. Instead, what we've learned from research in embodied cognition is that human intelligence seems to be a strongly integrated system with closely interconnected attributes, including emotions, desires, a strong sense of selfhood and autonomy, and a common sense understanding of the world. It's not at all clear that these attributes can be separated.

What is clear is that, to make and assess progress in AI more effectively, we will need to develop a better vocabulary for talking about what machines can do. And more generally, we will need a better scientific understanding of intelligence as it manifests in different systems in nature. This will require AI researchers to engage more deeply with other scientific disciplines that study intelligence.

Giving machines common sense will require imbuing them with the very basic 'core,' perhaps 'innate', knowledge that human infants possess about space, time, causality, and the nature of inanimate objects and other living agents, the ability to abstract from particular ideas to general concepts, and to make analogies from prior experience. No one yet knows how to capture such knowledge or abilities in machines. This is the current frontier of AI research, and one encouraging way forward is to tap into what is known about the development of these abilities in young children. Interestingly, this was the approach recommended by Alan Turing in his 1950 paper that introduced the Turing test. Turing suggested, "Instead of trying to produce a programme to simulate the adult mind, why not rather try to produce one which simulates the child's?"

CH3: AI: Types and technologies

"The sad thing about Artificial Intelligence is that it lacks artifice and therefore intelligence." - Jean Baudrillard

Perhaps the simplest way to distinguish between different types of AI is to call it either Narrow (weak) AI, or General (strong) AI. Specifically, there needs to be a key distinction made between complex and sophisticated systems, and systems that are capable of autonomy or human-like intelligence.

Narrow AI is what we see all around us in computers today -- intelligent systems that have been taught or have learned how to carry out specific tasks without being explicitly programmed how to do so.

There are a vast number of emerging applications for narrow AI:

- Interpreting video feeds from drones carrying out visual inspections of infrastructure such as oil pipelines.

- Organizing personal and business calendars.

- Responding to simple customer-service queries.

- Coordinating with other intelligent systems to carry out tasks like booking a hotel at a suitable time and location.

- Helping radiologists to spot potential tumours in X-rays.

- Flagging inappropriate content online.

- Generating a 3D model of the world from satellite imagery

- ... the list goes on and on.

New applications of these learning systems are emerging all the time. For example, graphics card designer Nvidia recently revealed an AI-based system Maxine, which allows people to make good quality video calls, almost regardless of the speed of their internet connection. The system reduces the bandwidth needed for such calls by a factor of 10 by not transmitting the full video stream over the internet and instead animating a small number of static images of the caller in a manner designed to reproduce the caller's facial expressions and movements in real-time and to be indistinguishable from the video.

However, as much untapped potential as these systems have, sometimes ambition for the technology outstrips reality. A case in point is self-driving cars, which themselves are underpinned by AI-powered systems such as computer vision. Electric car company Tesla is lagging some way behind CEO Elon Musk's original timeline for the car's Autopilot system, with the Full Self-Driving option only recently rolled out to a select group of expert drivers, as part of a beta testing program.

With narrow AI, whatever the program is meant to do, it is merely trying to replicate or duplicate that function, and for most tasks that is sufficient. Whereas general AI is an actual instantiation of that thing, which in this case is intelligence. Simply put, narrow AI simulates, whereas general AI just is.

Narrow AI is nothing new, it is the simulation of decision making. For example, the system that beat Kasparov at chess was calculating the best possible outcomes and making moves according to an algorithm. Here, we can say that the system was imitating intelligence by "thinking" about which move to make and then making it. While the system is playing chess, it is not actually thinking or deliberating about which move to make in the way that people might. This is far different from general AI, which is closer to decision making based on intelligence. Google's Deepmind system utilizes Machine Learning to learn from experience and makes autonomous decisions much like what we consider intelligence. Thus, it is general AI, or at least close.

General AI is meant to resemble the type of adaptable intellect found in humans; a flexible form of intelligence capable of learning how to carry out vastly different tasks. This is the sort of AI more commonly seen in movies, the likes of HAL in 2001 or Skynet in The Terminator, but which doesn't exist today – and AI experts are fiercely divided over how soon it will become a reality.

There are multiple benefits to AI machines having autonomy. Humans tend to think in a certain way, a way by which machines are not bound. Thus, AI systems can come up with unconventional solutions that humans would never conceive. In the future, AI systems will be able to offer solutions, not only to problems we cannot solve, but also to problems we are not even aware of. This is one of the major appeals of these types of systems: the ability to learn and surpass our problem-solving abilities.

Wide-ranging possibilities, such as computers matching or even exceeding human intelligence and capabilities on tasks such as complex decision-making; reasoning and learning; sophisticated analytics and pattern recognition; visual acuity; speech recognition and language translation; already exist, as do Smart Systems in communities; in vehicles; in buildings and utilities; on farms and in business processes; already and these will all save time, money and lives, offering opportunities for individuals to enjoy a more-customized future.

However, given the scepticism of leading lights in the field of modern AI and the very different nature of modern narrow AI systems to AGI (artificial general intelligence), there is perhaps little basis for fears that a general Artificial Intelligence will disrupt society in the near future.

Now that we've clarified that distinction, we can look at more sophisticated ways to differentiate between types of AI:

One typology differentiates AI systems based on the kind of intelligence they display. A second typology distinguishes AI applications based on the type of technology embedded into the AI system, whereas a third is based on the function performed by the AI.

- **Based on intelligence:**
  Philosophical debates on AI are centred on the notion of intelligent machines, that is machines that can learn, adapt and think like people. AI types based on such a notion fall in general

into three categories: artificial narrow intelligence, artificial general intelligence and artificial super intelligence.

While narrow (or weak) AI is usually able to solve only one specific problem and is unable to transfer skills from domain to domain, general AI aims for a human-level skill set. Once general AI is achieved, it is believed that it might lead to super intelligence that exceeds the cognitive performance of humans in virtually all domains of interest. This type of super intelligence can emerge following principles of evolution and complex adaptation. The argument states that if humans could create AI intelligence at a roughly human level, then this creation could, in turn, create yet higher intelligence and eventually evolve further. AI enthusiasts are providing estimates and outlining scenarios for when technological growth will reach the point of singularity and machine intelligence will surpass human intelligence. This raises philosophical arguments about the mind and the ethics of creating artificial beings endowed with human-like intelligence. Although the futuristic literature assumes that AI systems will be able to perform all tasks just as well as, or even better than, humans, this type of artificial general intelligence does not yet exist. There are, however, some AI programs, such as the GPT-3 language prediction application, that are beginning to exhibit some aspects of general intelligence.

- **Based on technology:**
  A second typology differentiates between the technologies embedded into the AI systems, which include Machine Learning, (its subclasses: Deep Learning and Reinforcement Learning), natural language processing, robots, various automation technologies (including robotic process automation), and rule-based Expert Systems (still in broad use although not considered a state-of-the-art technology). One recent survey suggests that all contemporary AI technologies (Machine Learning, Deep Learning, natural language processing) are either currently being used or will be used within a year by 95% or more of large adopters of AI.

26

- **Based on function:**

  This distinction differentiates between four types of AI: Conversational, Biometric, Robotic and Algorithmic. These categories overlap somewhat; for example, Conversational and Biometric AI already make extensive use of Algorithmic AI models, and Robotic AI is increasingly doing so.

  1. Conversational AI: refers to the general capability of computers to understand and respond to natural human language. Such systems include both voice and text-based technologies and vary largely based on their capability, domain and level of embodiment. Simple conversational AI is mainly used to handle repetitive client queries whereas smart conversational AI, enabled by Machine Learning and Natural Language Processing, has the potential to undertake more complex tasks that involve greater interaction, reasoning, prediction, and accuracy. Conversational AI has been used in many different fields; including finance, commerce, marketing, retail, and healthcare. Although the technology behind smart conversational agents is continuously developing, they currently do not have full human-level language abilities, sometimes resulting in misunderstanding and users' dissatisfaction.

  2. Biometric AI: relies on techniques to measure a person's physiological (fingerprints, hand geometry, retinas, iris, facial image) or behavioural (signature, voice, keystroke rhythms) traits. AI powered biometrics uses applications such as facial recognition, speech recognition and computer vision for identification, authentication and security objectives in computer devices, workplace and home security, among others. While fingerprints have the longest history as a marker of identity and continue to be used in several applications across the world, other bodily markers like face, voice, and iris or retina are proliferating, with significant research exploring their potential large-scale application. Meanwhile, the ubiquity

of face images and voice recordings, tagged with people's names on the Internet, alongside algorithms to transform such data into biometric recognition systems, has accelerated their use at a larger scale. Examples include identifying suspects, monitoring large events and surveillance of protests. Such large-scale use has triggered calls for regulation to introduce new laws, reform existing laws, or ban their use in some contexts.

3. Robotic AI: Physical robots have been used for many years to perform dedicated tasks in factory automation. Recently, AI including Machine Learning (ML) and Natural Language Processing (NLP), has become increasingly present in robotic solutions, enabling robots to move past automation and tackle more complex and high-level tasks. AI-enabled robots are equipped with the ability to sense their environment, comprehend, act, and learn. This helps robots perform a lot of tasks, from successfully navigating their surroundings, to identifying objects around them, or assisting humans with various tasks such as robotic-assisted surgeries.

4. Algorithmic AI: revolves around the use of Machine Learning (ML) algorithms— a set of unambiguous instructions that a mechanical computer can execute. Some ML algorithms can be trained on structured data and are specific to narrow task domains, such as speech recognition and image classification. Other algorithms, especially Deep Learning Neural Networks, are able to learn from large volumes of labelled data, enhance themselves by that learning and accomplish a variety of tasks such as classification, prediction and recognition. For example, a Neural Network can analyse the parameters of bank clients such as age, solvency, and credit history, and decide whether to approve a loan request. It can use face recognition to allow only authorized people into a building. On top of that, it can predict outcomes, such as the rise or fall of a stock based on past patterns and current data. Despite the potential

of ML algorithms, there are concerns that in some cases it might not be possible to explain how a system has reached its output. They might also be susceptible to introducing or perpetuating discriminatory bias.

Let's have a closer look at Machine Learning:

Most of what is labelled AI today, particularly in the public sphere, is actually Machine Learning (ML), a term in use for the past several decades. ML is an algorithmic field that blends ideas from statistics, computer science and many other disciplines to design algorithms that process data, make predictions, and help make decisions. In simple terms, Machine Learning is where a computer system learns how to perform a task rather than being programmed how to do so. To learn, these systems are fed huge amounts of data, which they then use to learn how to carry out a specific task, such as understanding speech or captioning a photograph. The quality and size of these datasets are important for building a system able to carry out its designated task accurately.

That ML would grow to have massive industrial relevance was already clear in the early 1990s and, by the turn of the century, forward-looking companies such as Amazon were already using ML throughout their business; solving mission-critical, back-end problems in fraud detection and supply-chain prediction, and building innovative consumer-facing services such as recommendation systems. As datasets and computing resources grew rapidly over the ensuing two decades, it became clear that ML would soon power not only Amazon but essentially any company in which decisions could be tied to large-scale data. New business models would emerge. The phrase 'Data Science' emerged to refer to this phenomenon; reflecting both the need of ML algorithms experts to partner with database and distributed systems experts to build scalable, robust ML systems and the larger social and environmental scope of the resulting systems. It is this confluence of ideas and technology trends that has been rebranded as 'AI' over the past few years.

AI, and, more specifically, Machine Learning, can be applied to identify patterns in nearly any dataset and in today's digital world we are awash with data. For Deep Learning, the more data the better. So to gather, learn and apply Machine Learning, AI systems exhibit some or all of the following qualities:

- Perception — Sensing the world through cameras, microphones, GPS, etc.
- Communication — Learning from interaction and gathering information based on action and response.
- Reasoning — Understanding concepts and relations between patterns in data.
- Decision making — Optimizing how to process the patterns in data to achieve specific outcomes.
- Interaction — Taking actions on these patterns to achieve specific goals.

Sixty years on, however, high-level reasoning and thought remain elusive. The developments now being called AI arose mostly in the engineering fields associated with low-level pattern recognition and movement control, as well as in the field of statistics: the discipline focused on finding patterns in data and on making well-founded predictions, tests of hypotheses, and decisions.

Indeed, the famous Backpropagation Algorithm that David Rumelhart rediscovered in the early 1980s, and which is now considered at the core of the so-called "AI revolution," first arose in the field of Control Theory in the 1950s and 1960s. One of its early applications was to optimize the thrusters of the Apollo spaceships as they headed towards the moon.

Some of the most heralded recent success stories of ML have, in fact, been in areas associated with Human-Imitative AI. Areas such as computer vision, speech recognition, game-playing, and robotics. Although one would not know it from reading the newspapers, success in this Human-Imitative AI has in fact been limited. The thrill (and fear) of making even limited progress on Human-Imitative AI gives rise to levels of over-exuberance and media attention that is not present in other areas of engineering.

In regular intervals since the 1950s, experts have predicted that it will only take a few years until we reach Artificial General Intelligence—systems that show behaviour indistinguishable from humans in all aspects and that have cognitive, emotional, and social intelligence.

In fact, the most powerful and profitable Artificial Intelligences we have produced, those of today's Machine Learning, exhibit a rather limited range of intelligent behaviour. Overwhelmingly, Machine Learning systems are oriented towards one specific task: to make accurate predictions. Drawing on statistical techniques that date back to the mid-20th century, Machine Learning theorists aim to develop algorithms that take a huge amount of data as input to a Neural Network and output a prediction rule or a classifier for the relevant domain in Polynomial-time (Polynomial-time algorithms are considered to be efficient, as opposed to exponential-time algorithms which grow much more rapidly as the problem size increases).

So what are these Neural Networks?

The key to Machine Learning success is Neural Networks. These mathematical models can tweak internal parameters to change what they output. A Neural Network is fed datasets that teach it what it should spit out when presented with certain data during training.

The structure and functioning of Neural Networks is very loosely based on the connections between neurons in the brain. Neural networks are made up of interconnected layers of algorithms that feed data into each other. They can be trained to carry out specific tasks by modifying the importance attributed to data as it passes between these layers. During the training of these Neural Networks, the weights attached to data as it passes between layers will continue to be varied until the output from the Neural Network is very close to what is desired. At that point, the network will have 'learned' how to carry out a particular task.

A subset of Machine Learning is Deep Learning, where Neural Networks are expanded into sprawling networks with many sizeable layers that are trained using massive amounts of data. These Deep Neural Networks have fuelled the current leap forward in the ability of computers to carry out tasks like speech recognition and computer vision.

There are various types of Neural Networks with different strengths and weaknesses:

- Recurrent Neural Networks (RNN) are a type of neural net particularly well suited to Natural Language Processing (NLP) -- understanding the meaning of text -- and speech recognition.

- Convolutional Neural Networks have their roots in image recognition and have uses as diverse as recommender systems and NLP.

- Long Short-Term Memory or LSTM - a type of recurrent Neural Network (RNN) architecture which uses sequential data or time series data making it particularly well suited to tasks such as Natural Language Processing and for stock market predictions – allowing it to operate fast enough to be used in on-demand systems like Google Translate.

- Evolutionary Algorithms can be used to optimize Neural Networks, resulting in Neuroevolution. It borrows from Darwin's theory of natural selection, seeing genetic algorithms undergo random mutations and combinations between generations in an attempt to evolve the optimal solution to a given problem. This approach has even been used to help design AI models, effectively using AI to help build AI. It could have an important role to play in helping design efficient AI as the use of intelligent systems becomes more prevalent, particularly as demand for data scientists often outstrips supply.

- Expert Neural Network systems are where computers are programmed with rules that allow them to take a series of decisions based on a large number of inputs, allowing that machine to mimic the behaviour of a human expert in a specific domain. An example of these knowledge-based systems might be, for example, an autopilot system flying a plane.

So how does Machine Learning work, you may be asking. For clarity Machine Learning is generally split into three main categories: Supervised, Unsupervised and Reinforcement Learning:

- **Supervised learning:**
  A common technique for teaching AI systems is by training them using many labelled examples. Machine Learning systems are fed huge amounts of data, annotated to highlight the features of interest. These might be photos labelled to indicate whether they contain a dog, or written sentences that have footnotes to indicate whether the word 'bass' relates to music or a fish. Once trained, the system can then apply these labels to new data, for example, to another image featuring a dog.

  This process of teaching a machine by example is called supervised learning. Labelling these examples is commonly carried out by online workers employed through platforms like Amazon Mechanical Turk. Training these systems typically requires vast amounts of data, with some systems needing to scour millions of examples to learn how to carry out a task effectively -although this is increasingly possible in an age of big data (data that is so large, fast or complex that it's difficult or impossible to process using traditional methods) and widespread data mining (the process of finding anomalies, patterns and correlations within large data sets to predict outcomes).

  Having access to huge, labelled datasets may also prove less important than access to large amounts of computing power in the long run. In recent years, Generative Adversarial Networks (GANs) have been used in machine-learning systems that only require a small amount of labelled data alongside a large amount of unlabelled data, which, as the name suggests, requires less manual work to prepare. This approach could allow for the increased use of semi-supervised learning, where systems can learn how to carry out tasks using a far smaller amount of labelled data than is necessary for training systems using supervised learning today.

- **Unsupervised learning:**
  In contrast, unsupervised learning uses a different approach, where algorithms try to identify patterns in data, looking for similarities that can be used to categorise that data. An example might be clustering together fruits that weigh a similar amount or cars with a similar engine size. The algorithm isn't set up in advance to pick out specific types of data; it simply looks for data that its similarities can group, for example, Google News grouping together stories on similar topics each day.

- **Reinforcement learning:**
  A crude analogy for reinforcement learning is rewarding a pet with a treat when it performs a trick. In reinforcement learning, the system attempts to maximise a reward based on its input data, basically going through a process of trial and error until it arrives at the best possible outcome.

  An example of reinforcement learning is Google DeepMind's Deep Q-network, which has been used to best human performance in a variety of classic video games. The system is fed pixels from each game and determines various information, such as the distance between objects on the screen. By also looking at the score achieved in each game, the system builds a model of which action will maximise the score in different circumstances, for instance, in the case of the video game Breakout, where the paddle should be moved to intercept the ball.

  The same approach is also used in robotics research, where reinforcement learning can help teach autonomous robots the optimal way to behave in real-world environments.

How close are we to creating human level intelligence? That's what you really want to know, right?

We can teach machines to learn in certain ways up to a point, but the barriers that separate machines from us and us from them, remain. When AI reaches mainstream usage, it is frequently no longer considered as such. This phenomenon is described as the AI Effect, which occurs when onlookers discount the behaviour of an AI program by arguing that it is not real intelligence. As the British science fiction writer Arthur C. Clarke once said, "Any sufficiently advanced technology is indistinguishable from magic." Yet when one understands the technology, the magic disappears.

If we look at the different levels of AI in terms of similarity to human intelligence, we can discern four separate types:

- **Type I AI: Reactive machines**
  The most basic types of AI systems are purely reactive and have the ability, neither to form memories, nor to use past experiences, to inform current decisions. Deep Blue, IBM's chess-playing supercomputer, which beat international grandmaster Garry Kasparov in the late 1990s, is the perfect example of this type of machine. Deep Blue can identify the pieces on a chess board and know how each moves. It can make predictions about what moves might be next for it and its opponent. And it can choose the most optimal moves from among the possibilities. Yet it doesn't have any concept of the past, nor any memory of what has happened before. Apart from a rarely used chess-specific rule against repeating the same move three times, Deep Blue ignores everything before the present moment. It simply looks at the pieces on the chess board as it stands right now and chooses from possible next moves.

  This type of intelligence involves the computer perceiving the world directly and acting on what it sees. It doesn't rely on an internal concept of the world. The current intelligent machines we marvel at either have no such concept of the world or have a very limited and specialized one for the duties they are required to perform.

Similarly, Google's AlphaGo Zero, which has beaten top human Go experts, cannot evaluate all potential future moves. Its analysis method is more sophisticated than Deep Blue's, using a Neural Network to evaluate game developments, (it learned these games through trial-and-error or reinforcement - without human guidance, only playing games against itself). However, programmers still need to feed AlphaGo Zero an important piece of human knowledge: the rules of the game.

Chess and Go have explicit, finite, and stable goals, rules, and reward signals, which allow Machine Learning to be optimized. Most real-world managerial problems are far more complex than games like Chess or Go. For example, the rules of managerial problems might not be known, might be ambiguous, and/or might change over time. While AlphaGo Zero is impressive, it represents little, if any, progress toward artificial general intelligence.

These methods do improve the ability of AI systems to play specific games, but they cannot be easily changed or applied to other situations. These computerized imaginations have no concept of the wider world – meaning they cannot function beyond the specific tasks they are assigned and are easily fooled. They cannot interactively participate in the world, the way we imagine AI systems one day might. Instead, these machines will behave in the same way every time they encounter the same situation. This can be very good for ensuring an AI system is trustworthy: You want your autonomous car to be a reliable driver. But it is bad if we want machines to truly engage with, and respond to, the world.

The phenomenon of "catastrophic forgetting" explains this machine limitation; that is, having learned one task and subsequently transferred to another, a machine-learning system simply "forgets" how to perform the previously learned task.

Humans, on the other hand, possess the capacity to transfer learning, allowing them to generalize from one task context to another. These simplest of AI systems won't ever be bored, or interested, or sad.

- **Type II AI: Limited memory**
  This class contains machines that can look into the past. Self-driving cars do some of this already. For example, they observe other cars' speed and direction. That cannot be done in just one moment, but rather requires identifying specific objects and monitoring them over time. These observations are added to the self-driving cars' preprogramed representations of the world, which also include lane markings, traffic lights and other important elements, like curves in the road. They're included when the car decides when to change lanes, to avoid cutting off another driver or being hit by a nearby car.

  However, these simple pieces of information about the past are only transient. They aren't saved as part of the car's library of experience it can learn from, the way human drivers compile experience over years behind the wheel. So how can we build AI systems that build full representations, remember their experiences and learn how to handle new situations? Research into methods inspired by Darwinian evolution can start to make up for human shortcomings by letting the machines build their own representations.

- **Type III AI: Theory of mind**
  We might stop here, and call this point the important divide between the machines we have and the machines we will build in the future. Machines in the next, more advanced, class not only form representations about the world, but also about other agents or entities in the world. In psychology, this is called "theory of mind" – the understanding that people, creatures and objects

in the world can have thoughts and emotions that affect their own behaviour.

This is crucial to how we humans formed societies because they allowed us to have social interactions. Without understanding each other's motives and intentions, and without considering what somebody else knows either about me or the environment, working together is at best difficult, at worst impossible.

If AI systems are indeed ever to walk among us, they'll have to be able to understand that each of us has thoughts and feelings and expectations for how we'll be treated. And they'll have to adjust their behaviour accordingly.

- **Type IV AI: Self-awareness**
  The final step of AI development is to build systems that can form representations about themselves. Ultimately, we AI researchers will have to not only understand consciousness but build machines that have it. Conscious beings are aware of themselves, know about their internal states, and can predict the feelings of others. We assume someone sounding their horn behind us in traffic is angry or impatient, because that's how we feel when we do the same thing to others. Without a theory of mind, we could not make those sorts of inferences.

  To reach this goal, we must focus our efforts toward understanding memory, learning and the ability to base decisions on past experiences. This is an important step toward understanding human intelligence on its own and it is crucial if we want to design or evolve machines that are more than just exceptional at classifying what they see in front of them.

CH4: AI: World Importance

"Anything that could give rise to smarter-than-human intelligence—in the form of Artificial Intelligence, brain-computer interfaces, or neuroscience-based human intelligence enhancement – wins hands down beyond contest as doing the most to change the world. Nothing else is even in the same league." - Eliezer Yudkowsky

Artificial intelligence has started generating significant economic value. With algorithms that make predictions from large amounts of data, AI contributes, by some estimates, about $2 trillion to today's global economy. It could add as much as $16 trillion by 2030, making it more than 10 percent of gross world product. AI's outsize contribution to global economic growth has important implications for geopolitics. Around the world, governments are ramping up their investments in AI research and development, infrastructure, talent, and product development. As at 2023, twenty-four governments have published national AI strategies and their corresponding investments.

So far, China and the United States are outspending everyone else, while simultaneously taking steps to protect their investments from foreign competition. In 2017, China passed legislation requiring foreign companies to store data from Chinese customers within China's borders, effectively preventing outsiders from using Chinese data to offer services to non-Chinese parties. For its part, the U.S. Committee on Foreign Investment, blocked a Chinese investor from acquiring a leading U.S. producer of semiconductors, which are essential components for computing. While this was officially a national security action, it also benefits U.S competitiveness by protecting its stake in semiconductor production.

The extent to which countries participate in this value chain will determine how they fare in the emerging global economic order and the stability of the broader international system. Indeed, if the gains from AI are distributed in highly variable ways, extreme divergence in national outcomes could drive widespread instability.

Machine learning, the science of having computers make decisions without being explicitly programmed, is the subfield of AI responsible for the majority of technical advances and economic investment. In recent years, Machine Learning has led all categories of AI patents (and constituted the third fastest-growing category of all patents granted, behind 3D printing and e-cigarettes) and attracted nearly 60 percent of all investment in AI.

To understand how AI contributes to the economy we need to look at value chains. A value chain describes the sequence of steps through which companies take raw materials and add value to them, resulting in a finished, commercially viable product. For Machine Learning, that value chain consists of five stages: data collection, data storage, data preparation, algorithm training, and application development.

- **Data Collection:**
  Raw data is the bedrock of Machine Learning. Every day, roughly 2.5 quintillion (1 followed by 18 zeros) bytes of raw data are collected via myriad devices, from tactile sensors to system logs, that record all manner of digital transactions, such as internet searches, camera images, phone calls, social media posts, and credit card transactions. With data collection increasingly taking place through mobile devices, it's no surprise that China and India are two of the most significant data collectors in the world.

  The number of mobile device users is a useful estimate of how much and from where, data is collected worldwide. In absolute terms, China and India have the most mobile device users with 1.22 and 0.44 billion users, respectively. These two countries also contribute the most to Asia's impressive number of internet users, which exceeded 2 billion in 2018—roughly the same number of internet users in the other six regions combined (Asian part of Russia, Central, Western, Southern, Eastern and South-eastern Asia).

The U.S. and European mobile markets are almost saturated at 97.1 and 93.6 mobile broadband subscriptions per 100 users, respectively. The Middle East, Asia and the Pacific regions are hovering at around 70 subscriptions per 100 users, leaving a sizable margin for further growth. Africa is lagging behind with an average of 29.7 subscriptions per 100 users, but this shortfall presents a significant economic opportunity for African countries seeking to expand their data collection capacity.

- **Data Storage:**
  Once data are collected, they are stored and secured in data centres. In the early days of Machine Learning, companies stored their data in their own bricks and mortar data centres that contained room-size computer servers. But data storage is increasingly shifting to the cloud, where companies access their data through the internet from cloud service providers that operate hundreds of servers and thousands of virtual machines. The most advanced means of data storage today - hyperscale data centres, or HDCs - operate thousands of servers and millions of virtual machines across multiple locations.

  To keep pace with the unprecedented volume of data collected every day, the data storage market is expanding. The United States dominates the market - 40 percent of HDCs are located there or owned by U.S. companies. China, Japan, and the United Kingdom together account for 20 percent of the market. Because HDCs require significant amounts of energy to operate, countries with low electricity costs may be able to secure a foothold in the HDC market.

- **Data Preparation:**
  Unlike data storage, which is capital intensive, data preparation is labour intensive. Raw data are generally messy and unstructured, containing numerous outliers and errors. Highly skilled data

41

engineers and scientists are needed to clean the data and convert them into a usable format (usually a table of seemingly endless rows and columns), a practice called data pre-processing. Less-skilled human reviewers, or 'data labellers,' also may be employed to manually classify a subset of the pre-processed data depending on the type of algorithm deployed.

Demand for highly skilled data scientists and less skilled data labellers will increase. The market for data labelling may provide an especially low barrier to entry for countries where English is not the first language, because many of the common tasks involved in data labelling, like image classification, merely require digital literacy rather than English literacy.

- **Algorithm Training:**
  Once the data are prepared, companies can start training their algorithms to make predictions on new data. With dozens of algorithm types and nearly infinite configurations to choose from, they require data scientists to develop alternative models and compare their prediction performance, making highly skilled labour a fundamental input to algorithm development and training. Another fundamental input is computer hardware: the most sophisticated algorithms that make predictions from big datasets involve trillions of calculations together with machines made of bespoke semiconductors that can perform such computations quickly and efficiently.

  Beyond the United States' almost unchallenged leadership in some of the key components that power the algorithm-training node of the AI economy, a handful of other countries - namely Japan, South Korea, Germany, and the United Kingdom - are shoring up their positions by boosting investment in R&D and STEM education (science, technology, engineering, and mathematics).

- **Application Development:**
  Algorithmic predictions are translated into actionable insights via applications—software programs developed by software engineers, or app developers. The potential applications of Machine Learning algorithms are nearly endless, ranging from personal assistants (such as Amazon's Alexa) to product recommendations (for example, YouTube's video recommender) to autonomous weapons (like military drones).

  Country engagement in the app market is especially important because apps, mobile or otherwise, generate additional user data that will continually expand the database on which Machine Learning algorithms can train, leading to more accurate predictions and more valuable products. Looking regionally, Asia and the Pacific (33 percent), Europe (30 percent), and North America (29 percent), hold roughly similar shares of the mobile app developer market.

Geopolitical Implications:

China and the United States, are heavily investing across most, if not all, parts of the Machine Learning value chain - effectively ensuring that both economies will triumph in the so-called race to win AI. Moderate movers, by contrast, are concentrating their investments in particular nodes of the value chain. Germany, Japan, and Taiwan, for instance, are heavily investing in the physical capital required for data storage and algorithm training (like HDCs and supercomputers). Australia and South Korea are investing in the requisite intellectual capital (for example, R&D and STEM graduates).

Concentrating talent and wealth in certain countries will likely exacerbate economic inequality between countries. A similar geographical concentration of talent and wealth in certain cities could also impact land and housing prices, causing demographic shifts.

Let's look at an example of how international competition in AI development is contributing to globally significant concerns:

China has very recently developed an 'AI Ship Designer' which, they claim, works at unprecedented speed; performing a year's work in only 24 hours.

A team of Chinese researchers funded by China's People's Liberation Army (PLA) are claiming to have used Artificial Intelligence (AI) to design an electrical layout of a warship with 100 percent accuracy and at an unprecedented speed.

A team of researchers from the China Ship Design and Research Centre, headed by Luo Wei, a senior engineer, published a paper in the Chinese-language journal Computer Integrated Manufacturing Systems on February 27th 2023. In it the researchers claimed that their AI designer took only a day to complete work that humans would need nearly a year to achieve with the most advanced computer tools.

Considering the scale and complexity of modern warships, mistakes are sure to happen during the design process, and it can take several hours to discover and rectify them. However, when the researchers put the AI designer to the test, with more than 400 challenging tasks, they found that the AI could accomplish 100 percent accuracy.

According to the researchers, while there is still room for improvement, their AI designer was "ready for engineering applications" in China's shipbuilding industry to increase the rate of warship manufacturing. Luo's team said that the Chinese military funded their AI designer project because the design process was the main area hindering the speed of production of warships rather than shipyard delays.

Chinese AI Compared To That Of Google

Luo's team compared their AI designer to those developed by companies like Google to increase the speed of computer chip design. There were some interesting and, perhaps, critical differences between the two.

Firstly, the team notes in the paper that there is no room for error in warship design, and the AI chip designer can make a few mistakes.Furthermore, the team said that while an AI chip designer could produce many products, computing resources could be assigned to train it, and the company could still realize a profit margin. Whereas their AI warship designer was only working on one vessel without the resources of a Big Tech company.

Also, unlike an AI system that learns and makes decisions independently without human intervention, the warship designer created by the team is a machine that operates with human guidance. The AI designer starts by consulting a database of Chinese ship design knowledge and experience from past decades, and then it comes up with a design, which it checks against the database. According to Luo's team, this approach significantly reduced the computing resources needed and eliminated errors.

The team also noted that the AI designer's effectiveness had only been proven for the layout of electrical systems. However, it also carried out these design tasks much faster and more accurately than humans, and it could be used easily with a small computer system.

The global significance of this development

China already boasts the world's largest navy numerically, after overtaking the US Navy between 2015 and 2020. If the recent claims by Luo's team are anything to go by, the US military planners have much to fear.

The US is already concerned about China's expanding naval fleet and its capacity to produce warships at a very high pace. The US Navy Secretary Carlos Del Toro, told reporters in Washington in March 2023 that US naval shipyards cannot match the output of Chinese ones.

"They have 13 shipyards. One of those shipyards has more capacity than all of our shipyards combined. That presents a real threat," Del Toro said.

China intends to build a fleet of more than 400 warships by 2025. The US naval fleet is currently under 300 ships, and the Pentagon aims to have 350 manned vessels by 2045 - still way behind China.

In January 2023, a senior American naval expert, Sam Tangredi, a former US Navy captain and the Leidos Chair of Future Warfare Studies at the US Naval War College, warned that the US Navy might lose to China's PLA Navy, which enjoys a substantial numerical advantage over the US, saying, "the side with the most ships almost always wins."

In a January 2023 issue of the US Naval Institute's (USNI's) Proceedings magazine, Tangredi looked at 28 naval wars in history, going back to the Greco-Persian Wars of 500 BC, and found that superior technology defeated more significant numbers in only three instances.

On the issue of a potential future conflict with China, Tangredi said that a naval war against China in the western Pacific in this decade would see a smaller US Naval force against a gigantic PLA Navy, and that too in waters near China, inside the range of PLA's air and rocket forces.

"US leaders must ask themselves to what extent they are willing to bet on technological—without numerical—superiority in that fight," wrote Tangredi.

CH5: AI: Benefits

"Some people worry that Artificial Intelligence will make us feel inferior, but then, anybody in his right mind should have an inferiority complex every time he looks at a flower." - Alan Kay (inventor of the world's first portable notebook)

Artificial intelligence is pervasive in our lives, whether we realize it or not. One of the most public uses of AI is in driverless cars, which have been approved for road operation in five American states as well as the District of Columbia and there are no signs of that growing industry slowing down. New developments, such as these cars, have prompted an AI arms race in the private sector.

If we consider that the internet today is worth $50 trillion, it is not difficult to see how you could extrapolate that to at least three or four times as many applications to get figures as high as $200 trillion. Could it be any less with AI having so many different industries and applications? Everything that is currently on the internet can also be manifested through AI in smarter, better and more effective ways.

The desire for robots to be able to act autonomously, understand and navigate the world around them means there is a natural overlap between robotics and AI. While AI is only one of the technologies used in robotics, it is helping robots learn new skills and move into new areas, such as self-driving cars and delivery robots. At the start of 2020, General Motors and Honda revealed the Cruise Origin, an electric-powered driverless car and Waymo, the self-driving group inside Google parent Alphabet, recently opened its Robotaxi service to the general public in Phoenix, Arizona, covering a 50-square mile area in the city.

After a successful trial, the world's first driverless buses have been launched in Edinburgh in the spring of 2023 as part of a project that will see these automated vehicles travel along a 14-mile route at up to 50mph. The buses are operated by Stagecoach who are aiming to put five of the automated vehicles in service between Fife and Edinburgh. Sensors on the buses allow them to run on pre-determined routes without a driver needing to control them. They have undergone trials at a depot as well as track testing and virtual simulation. The first road test has now been carried out with a group of volunteers becoming the first in the UK to travel on a full-size, self-driving bus, on a public road.

All these autonomous vehicles—cars, trucks, buses, and drone delivery systems—use advanced technological capabilities. Those features include automated vehicle guidance and braking, lane-changing systems, the use of cameras and sensors for collision avoidance, the use of AI to analyse information in real time, and the use of high-performance computing and Deep Learning systems to adapt to new circumstances through detailed maps. Advanced software enables cars to learn from the experiences of other vehicles on the road and adjust their guidance systems as weather, driving, or road conditions change.

Ride-sharing companies are very interested in autonomous vehicles. They see advantages in terms of customer service and labour productivity. All the major ride-sharing companies are exploring driverless cars. The surge of car-sharing and taxi services—such as Uber and Lyft in the United States, Daimler's Mytaxi and Hailo service in Great Britain, and Didi Chuxing in China - demonstrate the opportunities for this transportation option. Uber recently signed an agreement to purchase 24,000 autonomous cars from Volvo for its ride-sharing service. However, Uber suffered a setback in March 2018 when one of its autonomous vehicles in Arizona hit and killed a pedestrian. They and several auto manufacturers immediately suspended testing and launched investigations into what went wrong and how the fatality occurred. Both industry and consumers want reassurance that the technology is safe and able to deliver on its stated promises. Unless there are persuasive answers, this accident could slow AI advancements in the transportation sector.

Machine-learning systems have helped computers recognise what people are saying with an accuracy of almost 95%. Microsoft's Artificial Intelligence and Research group also reported it had developed a system that transcribes spoken English as accurately as human transcribers.

With researchers pursuing a goal of 99% accuracy, we can expect speaking to computers to become increasingly common, alongside more traditional forms of human-machine interaction.

Meanwhile, Open AI's Language Prediction Model GPT-3 recently caused a stir with its ability to create articles that could pass as being written by a human.

The success of GPT-3 (now thought to have the fastest-growing user base of any application in history), has spawned an outpouring of tool development, which has the potential to make life easier in a range of different ways. For example:

- Synthesia:
  Allows anyone to create branded videos and corporate content and see it brought to life in front of their eyes by AI avatars. This is a form of synthetic video that can vastly reduce the amount of time businesses spend filming and editing content. If changes need to be made, the scripts can simply be edited, and the video will be updated. It also automatically handles translation into over 120 languages.

- Cleanvoice:
  Automates the clean-up of audio and vocal tracks by removing background noise, stuttering, "ums and errs," as well as dead airtime and lengthy silences to create clean, professional-sounding recordings.

- Jasper:
  An AI copywriting tool that works in a similar fashion to ChatGPT and is based on the same GPT-3 language model. However, it is

more tuned toward creating advertising and marketing copy rather than acting as a conversational interface.

- Pictory:
This is a tool for taking long-form video content and quickly creating branded, shareable clips without requiring any technical editing experience, or even transforming blog posts into videos. It works by finding the most valuable and engaging moments and automatically combining them with voiceovers, stock footage, and music.

- Canva:
A very popular cloud-based online design tool and Canva subscribers now have access to Magic Write, an AI-driven copywriting tool. From a simple prompt, it can create social posts, blog outlines, lists, content suggestions, captions, and more.

- Upscaler:
A free tool provided by the stockphotos.com image bank that automatically upscales and enhances images, meaning that low-resolution pictures can be magnified without losing detail. The FacePro feature is particularly suited to facial images.

- Taplio:
This is a tool specifically designed to work with LinkedIn to help with creating, scheduling, and posting content, building relationships with your network and new contacts and monitoring the impression your posts are making. The AI assists by providing inspiration for posts and stories.

- Picsart
A text-to-image platform with a comprehensive set of image-editing tools that lets you turn words into art and then fine-tune the results to get the images that you need.

- Talk To Books:

This is an experimental ChatGPT-style conversational interface plugged into the Google Books library, capable of surfacing facts, quotes, and passages from literature. You can filter categories of books so asking, for example, a historical question will only return answers contained in historical fiction or non-fiction.

- KeywordInsights:
  AI-powered insights into the keywords you need to be targeting to ensure your search engine optimization campaigns are hitting the right notes. Automatically clusters keywords and determines search intent so you can see what terms are valuable and what is just 'noise'.

- Sprinklr:
  Social listening enhanced by AI – understand what your customers or audience is saying about your brand and automatically draw out insights from millions of conversations taking place all over the world. Analyze the sentiment of your mentions and tap into new audiences wherever they are.

- Lisa AI Art – Magic Avatar:
  Android app that lets users tap into AI effects to enhance the look of social profile pictures and avatars to attract more interaction and engagement.

- Perplexity.ai:
  Another GPT-3 powered chatbot interface, but this time focused on delivering accurate answers to complex questions. Unlike ChatGPT, it is happy to reveal the source of the information it uses, making it more useful for many kinds of research.

What about the roles AI plays in your day-to-day routine?

- Your morning commute: Google Maps uses location data and Neural Networks to calculate the best route and predict your arrival time. Ride hailing apps such as Uber and Lyft use Machine Learning to calculate dynamic pricing based on demand.

- Your communications: Depending on your email provider, most are using AI to keep spam out of your inbox, while social media platforms such as Facebook use Machine Learning for recommendations and face matching to help with tagging friends in photos. Natural Language Processing is now more powerful than ever, with Open AI's GPT-3 as a most recent example of powerful Neural Networks which can understand, create, and translate languages.

- Your shopping experience: Using cookies (identifying tags that are placed on your phone or computer when browsing the web), AI learns what you like and serves you up relevant and timely ads. Whether shopping online or in the real world, AI and technologies such as augmented reality and image recognition are being used to help you pick the best outfit. Then when you make a purchase, AI protects you from fraud.

- Relaxing at home: Smart home technology has come a long way from AI powered locks and thermostats, lights and music. AI assistants like Alexa and Google Home help to connect it all together, learning when you arrive home and setting the temperature and lights accordingly. As far as entertainment is concerned, Netflix's recommendation engine learns from you and people like you to predict which shows you will binge next, while video games push the limits of AI to create realistic virtual experiences.

- Relaxing at work: Since Covid-19, many of us have been commuting to our living rooms. In many ways, AI has helped us transition to remote work through AI-powered applications and digital tools. Whether it is automating customer service support, scheduling your next meeting, or optimizing your video conference, AI is likely involved. For those who are still on the factory floor, automated processes and robots are taking away much of the strain of menial tasks.

What about the bigger picture?

Economy:

One of the reasons for the growing role of AI is the tremendous opportunities for economic development that it presents. A project undertaken by Price Waterhouse Cooper, estimated that Artificial Intelligence technologies could increase global GDP by $15.7 trillion, a full 14%, by 2030. That includes advances of $7 trillion in China, $3.7 trillion in North America, $1.8 trillion in Northern Europe, $1.2 trillion for Africa and Oceania, $0.9 trillion in the rest of Asia outside of China, $0.7 trillion in Southern Europe, and $0.5 trillion in Latin America. China is making rapid strides because it has set a national goal of investing $150 billion in AI and becoming the global leader in this area by 2030.

Finance:

Investments in financial AI in the United States tripled between 2013 and 2014 to a total of $12.2 billion. According to observers in that sector, decisions about loans are now being made by software that can consider a variety of finely parsed data about a borrower, rather than just a credit score and a background check. In addition, there are so-called robo-advisers that create personalized investment portfolios, obviating the need for stockbrokers and financial advisers. These advances are designed to take the emotion out of investing and undertake decisions based on analytical considerations, making these choices in a matter of minutes.

Criminal justice:

AI is being deployed in the criminal justice area. The city of Chicago has developed an AI-driven 'Strategic Subject List' that analyses people who have been arrested, for their risk of becoming future perpetrators. It ranks 400,000 people on a scale of 0 to 500, using items such as age, criminal activity, victimization, drug arrest records, and gang affiliation. In looking at the data, analysts found that youth is a strong predictor of violence, being a shooting victim is associated with becoming a future perpetrator, gang affiliation has little predictive value, and drug arrests are not significantly associated with future criminal activity.

Judicial experts claim AI programs reduce human bias in law enforcement which leads to a fairer sentencing system. However, critics worry that AI algorithms represent a secret system to punish citizens for crimes they haven't yet committed. The risk scores have been used numerous times to guide large-scale roundups. The fear is that such tools target people of colour unfairly and have not helped Chicago reduce the murder wave that has plagued it in recent years.

Despite these concerns, other countries are moving ahead with rapid deployment in this area. In China, for example, companies already have considerable resources and access to voices, faces and other biometric data in vast quantities, which would help them develop their technologies. New technologies make it possible to match images and voices with other types of information, and to use AI on these combined data sets to improve law enforcement and national security. Through its "Sharp Eyes" program, Chinese law enforcement is matching video images, social media activity, online purchases, travel records, and personal identity. This integrated database enables authorities to keep track of criminals, potential lawbreakers and terrorists. Put differently, China has become the world's leading AI-powered surveillance state.

Global Warming:

As the size of machine-learning models and the datasets used to train them grows, so does the carbon footprint of the vast computing clusters that shape and run these models. The environmental impact of powering and cooling these computer farms was the subject of a paper by the World Economic Forum in 2018. One 2019 estimate was that the power required by machine-learning systems is doubling every 3.4 months.

The issue of the vast amount of energy needed to train powerful Machine Learning models was brought into focus recently by the release of the language prediction model GPT-3, a sprawling Neural Network with some 175 billion parameters. While the resources needed to train such models can be immense, and largely only available to major corporations, once trained, the energy needed to run these models is significantly less. However, as demand for services based on these models grows, power consumption and the resulting environmental impact again becomes an issue.

The argument that the environmental impact of training and running larger models needs to be weighed against the potential Machine Learning has to have a significant positive impact. The more rapid advances in healthcare that look likely following the breakthrough made by Google DeepMind's AlphaFold 2 serve as an important example.

Health Care:

AI could eventually have a dramatic impact on healthcare, helping radiologists pick out tumours in x-rays, aiding researchers in spotting genetic sequences related to diseases and identifying molecules that could lead to more effective drugs. The recent breakthrough by Google's AlphaFold 2 machine-learning system is expected to reduce the time taken to complete a key step when developing new drugs from months to hours.

There have been trials of AI-related technology in hospitals across the world. These include IBM's Watson clinical decision support tool, which is trained by oncologists at Memorial Sloan Kettering Cancer Centre, and the use of Google DeepMind systems by the UK's National Health Service, where it will help spot eye abnormalities and streamline the process of screening patients for head and neck cancers.

There are many possible applications of AI in diagnosing and treating patients or helping senior citizens live fuller and healthier lives. But there is also enthusiasm about AI's role in contributing to broader public-health programs built around massive amounts of data that might be captured in the coming years, about everything from personal genomes to nutrition.

AI tools are helping designers improve computational sophistication in health care. For example, Merantix is a German company that applies Deep Learning to medical issues. It has an application in medical imaging that detects lymph nodes in the human body in Computer Tomography (CT) images. According to its developers, the key is labelling the nodes and identifying small lesions or growths that could be problematic. Humans can do this, but radiologists charge $100 per hour and may be able to carefully read only four images an hour. If there were 10,000 images, the cost of this process would be $250,000, which is prohibitively expensive if done by humans.

What Deep Learning can do in this situation is train computers on data sets to differentiate between a normal-looking versus an irregular-appearing lymph node. After doing that through imaging exercises and honing the accuracy of the labelling, radiological imaging specialists can apply this knowledge to actual patients and determine the extent to which someone is at risk of cancerous lymph nodes. Since only a few are likely to test positive, it is a matter of identifying the unhealthy versus healthy node.

AI has been applied to congestive heart failure as well; an illness that afflicts 10 percent of senior citizens and costs $35 billion each year in the United States alone. AI tools are helpful because they predict in advance, potential challenges ahead and allocate resources to patient education, sensing, and proactive interventions that keep patients out of hospital.

Surgical robots have gained wide applicability in more than 1 million surgical procedures pertaining to orthopaedics, gynaecology, neurology, oncology and dentistry. AI has been used in conjunction with robots to aid in the precise withdrawal of blood from minute blood vessels during clinical procedures.

The amalgamation of AI with surgical robotics has enabled the exchange of important information between the surgical robots. In the future AI could aid surgeons in gaining access to real-time warnings and provide advice during procedures. Deep learning data could be utilized to render the best surgical practice with accuracy. However, this clinical AI requires further validation to achieve the best outcomes.

The enormous potential for improvements in healthcare via applications of AI are worth further consideration:

Applications of AI in Healthcare Drug Discovery:

One of the most important baselines for a pharmaceutical industry is drug discovery. The average time taken for a drug to reach the market is about 14 years, with a whopping cost of around $2.6 billion. The selection of a new successful drug from the cluster of prospective pharmacological active chemical entities (lead molecules), is the toughest task. With the help of AI, researchers can select a few clinically effective candidates out of thousands of molecules in a far smaller amount of time.

In 2015, there was an epidemic outbreak of Ebola virus in West Africa which struck many countries, killing 11,310 people. At this point there was an urgent need for a drug which could be used for treatment. An AI-powered program provided by a company called Atomwise was used to screen the drugs available. The company then collaborated with the Toronto University and IBM to identify a treatment for the virus infections. The drugs were made in a reduced span of time allowing a global pandemic to be avoided.

After the discovery of a drug, it generally takes 4.5-5 years for it to reach clinical trials stage. Astonishingly, in 2019 a Japan based pharmaceutical company, Sumitomo Dainippon Pharma, which had a collaboration with UK based biotech Exscientia, designed a new drug using AI for the treatment of OCD (obsessive-compulsive disorder). It was the first in the medical world to design a drug using AI right from scratch. The task which normally takes 4.5 years was achieved within 12 months.

Machine learning has also been explored for the identification of potential antibiotics from a list of 100 million molecules. As antibiotic resistance is on the rise and is a threat to millions of people, scientists are working on ways to overcome this challenge. AI has been explored by scientists in studying the DNA sequences which are responsible for causing antibiotic resistance.

The next blockbuster drug could be invented by Artificial Intelligence:

For years, billions of dollars have been poured into bringing AI into the drug development process. Finally, it seems the cash might be paying off.

Medicines designed by AI for conditions including lymph cancers, inflammatory diseases and motor neurone diseases are reaching trials in humans. For many, it's just a matter of time before they're sitting on the shelf in a pharmacy.

If successful, AI promises nothing less than a revolution for the pharmaceutical industry: As well as dramatically reducing the time it takes to develop a new medicine, it could help identify new drug molecules that have so far eluded scientists. Drugmakers would pocket billions of dollars, but it would also mean patients could have access to new, innovative drugs at a pace not seen before.

But years of waiting for a result have left some sceptical that AI will deliver. While investors have been thronging to the space, no doubt spurred on by promises of a potential multi-billion opportunity, that won't continue if AI-developed drugs don't come to market.

And there's still one significant hurdle to overcome: The availability of data.

The premise for using AI in drug discovery and development is pretty straightforward: Use algorithms to trawl through vast troves of data - including the structures of chemical compounds, animal studies and information from patients - to help identify what a future drug needs to target in the human body; which molecule would be best suited for this; and most enticingly, how to create new molecules altogether.

"I absolutely believe that all drugs will be designed this way in the future, because it's a far more efficient way to design molecules," said Andrew Hopkins, the founder of Exscientia, which was one of the first companies to blaze onto the space in 2012. "The question is, how fast will the industry adopt this?", he said.

But with high profile failures, such as the near collapse of Sensyne Health and IBM's Watson not living up to its big ambitions, there's a lingering sense that AI might not meet the hype when it comes to developing new drugs.

Currently, all eyes are on whether AI-designed medicines will be safe for people, will have the desired effect on the disease and will be able to meet the rigorous regulatory standards required to actually be approved for human use.

"In the next few years, we need to see clinical success of AI-driven projects, otherwise there will be a problem with translation to efficacy and safety of methods," said Andreas Bender, Professor of Molecular Informatics at Cambridge University and co-founder of AI drug discovery companies Healx and Pharmenable.

Jim Weatherall, AstraZeneca's vice president of data science, AI and R&D, says the challenge for the next few years is getting AI designed and developed drugs through the regulatory process. If patients are actually going to benefit from these drugs, they need to receive them - which means the drugs will need to pass through the same regulatory hoops as traditional medicines.

With multiple AI-designed drugs now being tested on humans, it could soon be crunch time.

Exscientia was first out of the blocks in 2020 with a drug it hoped could treat obsessive compulsive disorder. While that study was discontinued after failing to reach expected criteria, the company now has a cancer drug and one for inflammatory diseases in clinical trials.

And it's not the only one. Schrödinger has a potential lymphoma drug in clinical trials, Insilico has a drug to treat idiopathic pulmonary fibrosis that's expected to enter phase 2 trials in 2023, and Verge Genomics is trialling a novel therapeutic for amyotrophic lateral sclerosis (ALS).

In some cases, such as with Verge's ALS drug, the drug development process itself has been thrown on its head. Traditionally, drugs are tested in animals before moving to humans. Instead, Verge's platform uses human data and human models in the discovery and development phase, a process that they believe provides more insightful findings than animal models.

But it's not a given that the first AI-drug approval will open the proverbial floodgates. In different disease areas, there are different targets and different chemistry, meaning things can look entirely different. If there's success with one drug there will probably be public hype and more money coming into the area, but that doesn't mean that all future projects are more likely to be successful.

What's needed is a better understanding of which data is predictive and meaningful in which disease context, to know which tool will be useful, in which situation and that means data - lots of it.

For a drug to even make it to clinical trials, the AI systems need be able to design it. To do that, they need access to immense quantities of data. That includes everything from data on the chemical composition of different molecules, to research papers and patient data. Without access to good quality and extensive data, the AI systems will not provide the most accurate results.

For a smaller company like the Italian biotech Dompé, that can be a major hurdle. "The new gap for me and a vision right now is the generation of high quality data in an amount that unlocks the true potential of Artificial Intelligence Deep Learning. These techniques require a massive amount of validated data," said Andrea Beccari, who heads up Dompé's drug discovery platform.

A company like Dompé will not be able to do work at the scale of a large U.S. pharmaceutical company, but if there were a central repository of data, Beccari believes this could be a gamechanger for Europe - something like the European Health Data Space (EHDS) currently being negotiated by the European Parliament.

The EHDS proposal seeks to make access to data for research much easier through the implementation of a system whereby researchers can request particular datasets through a permit. This could be data held by a public authority or even a pharmaceutical company, helping to level the playing field.

The EHDS promises to help create standards, improve interoperability and allow access to endless datasets. AstraZeneca's Weatherall acknowledges that the opportunity is tremendous, but says that the key is to achieve this without overbearing bureaucracy.

While AI promises to revolutionize the industry, those working on it for decades don't see it as an algorithm doing all the work. Rather, it's about "human in the loop AI," said Weatherall. So, yes, it's a new way of working, but it just includes a few more experts in the room. Those experts are increasingly being tapped on by Big Pharma. Industry is hedging its bets to ensure it's not left in the wake of biotech startups that are flooding the space. Consultancy McKinsey estimates there are nearly 270 companies working in AI-driven drug discovery. While the majority are in the U.S., there are hubs emerging in Western Europe and Southeast Asia.

In 2022, Pfizer extended its collaboration with an Israeli AI company; AstraZeneca expanded its cooperation with Benevolent AI; and Sanofi announced new work with Exscientia as well as a deal with Insilico Medicine.

In addition to partnerships like the one with Benevolent AI, British-Swedish drugmaker AstraZeneca has an in-house team of experts that are applying AI extensively in the drug discovery process. Ola Engkvist, associate director of computational chemistry, discovery sciences and R&D at AstraZeneca has suggested that AI tools are applied to around 70 percent of the company's drug discovery projects focused on small molecules (traditional drugs made from chemical compounds) and that they are also starting to use it in more complex projects such as antibody design.

Engkvist's AstraZeneca colleague Weatherall believes that AI is the future of drug development. "We've been on a journey from 'what is this?' to 'why did we ever do it any other way?'" he said.

Boost in clinical trials:

Between the years 2000 and 2015, the success rates for clinical trials were quite low. It was reported that only 13.8% of candidates could successfully get through all three stages of clinical trials. After the implementation of AI, the cycle time has been reduced whilst, at the same time, productivity costs are lower and outcomes improved. AI algorithms, along with digital infrastructures, enable a continuous stream of clinical trial data to be coded, stored, and managed. Alongside this, electronic data capture is being used in an improved manner, for the reduction of human errors during the collection of data and seamless integration with other databases.

The technologies enabled with AI collect, organise and analyse the increasing amount of data generated by clinical trials, which includes the failed trials and helps in the extraction of meaningful patterns of information that aids with design. Details like EMR (electronic medical records) and medical images, which were collected through the physicians' notes: are utilized to determine the appropriate patients for the trial procedure. Additionally, it has become easier for patients, who can now convey the changes and other information through their smartphones and wearable devices. After monitoring the patients continuously and sharing the data across systems, all the data is consolidated on an analytics platform. A self- learning system has been designed to provide real-time insights about the safety and efficacy of the treatment and predict the dropouts risk, so that engagement and retention can be enhanced.

The use of AI-enabled health technologies and patient support platforms have been predicted to revolutionise clinical trials with improved success in the attraction, engagement and retention of committed patients throughout the study duration.

Digital consultation:

The concept of digital consultation is to reduce the hospital visits of patients for minor symptoms, which can be self-treated with the assistance of a medical practitioner within the comfort of the patients' home. There are now apps that use AI to provide the consultation, based on the patient's medical history (which can be found with a questionnaire that the patient is requested to complete) and general knowledge related to the medical field. The users are required to feed their symptoms into the app. The speech recognition system compares the symptoms provided by the patient with the databases of the illness. Then, recording the patient's medical history, the system recommends the course of action.

Remote patient monitoring:

The main source of expenditure in a hospital is manpower. To reduce this cost and at the same time provide patients with the required services, the concept of remote patient monitoring came into existence. As AI, sensors and predictive analysis are getting more advanced, there have been rapid developments in the concept of patient monitoring. Wearables and embedded sensors like glucometers and blood pressure monitors are already available. Other advances, like smart implants and smart prosthetics, are being used post -surgery, or for rehabilitation in patient management, avoiding post-operational complications by continuously monitoring the key parameters of the patient.

New and more advanced forms of patient monitoring are emerging. Digital pills, nanorobots and smart fabrics which help in monitoring medication adherence, wound management, and the monitoring of cardiac ailments are just three examples. They function by direct monitoring, which is enabled by brain-computer interfaces to measure vital health metrics to keep track of the patient's emotional, physiological, psychological and cognitive states. It is expected that by 2025, the market for patient monitoring, wearables and telehealth will be adopted by half the population in developed countries and will be worth more than $350 billion.

In a recent trial, the average cost to take care of 44 patients was $12,937. After the adoption of RPMS (Remote Patient Monitoring System), this dropped down to $1231.61. Thus, a 90% decrease in the cost of patient care was observed alongside a 95% patient adoption and overall patient satisfaction.

AI in nanotechnology research:

AI has been used in the simulations of nanoscale systems at an atomistic level. It can simulate the way a nanoparticle behaves and aid in the efficient selection of drug carriers cutting down the cost and labour involved in the development of nanoparticles.

As the field of nanomedicine has evolved over the years and continues to do so, several approaches have been adopted to deliver multiple therapeutic agents in fixed doses. A major challenge with this is that the effect of these drugs in unison depends on the time and dose and is specific to individual patients. AI could be effectively interfaced with nanomedicine in optimizing the dose to achieve an effective outcome, specifically in combination therapy.

Prediction of another epidemic outbreak:

Using the concept of Machine Learning, one form of AI, in which structured data points are used: like the location of the epidemic; the count of the reported cases in a particular time; the extent to which it is expanding, etc; can decide the extent of an outbreak. It also uses the data provided by social networking sites like Facebook, Instagram, Twitter, etc, where data is extracted through conversation groups or any forums where the users discuss the symptoms and cases in their areas or localities. Prediction is done using an algorithm which is created by compiling the data obtained from news broadcasts (in various languages), airline ticketing and also reports from tracking of the diseases in plants and animals. The algorithm thus created helps in predicting, or at least simulating, the speed of the disease.

A Canada based startup named BlueDot, which was founded in 2013 uses AI, Machine Learning and Big Data for tracking and predicting the outbreak of infectious diseases. Their engine collects data every 15 minutes throughout the day of more than 150 diseases and syndromes across the globe. The main aim of the engine is to contain the spread of contagious diseases. It collects the data provided by WHO and the Centre for Disease Control organizations and reports to private, government, healthcare and business sectors by providing them a brief synopsis of the disease outbreaks and the risks associated with it.

On the night of 30th December 2019, BlueDot spotted clusters of "unusual pneumonia" cases happening around the wet and dry markets of Wuhan, China. Immediately, BlueDot alerted their government and private sectors. This was later recognized as the novel coronavirus (COVID-19), which was reported to have infected lots of people across the globe and has emerged as a global pandemic.

The AI engine had already flagged Chinese articles reporting 27 cases of pneumonia which had a connection with the markets selling live animals and seafood in Wuhan. Apart from providing an alert, BlueDot had also accurately identified the cities that had connections with Wuhan, by analysing the data of global airline ticketing to identify the travelling of infected cases. It had already reported that international destinations like Tokyo, Singapore, Hong Kong, Phuket, Bangkok, Seoul, and Taipei had the highest number of travellers from Wuhan and that these cities would have a widespread number of cases. As anticipated, these were the top cities to be infected with COVID.

BlueDot has not only used their system for Corona virus, but have also applied it to predict the 2014 Ebola outbreak in West Africa and the spread of Zika virus to Florida in 2016, 6 months before it occurred.

These developments raise important policy, regulatory, and ethical issues. For example, how should we promote data access? How do we guard against biased or unfair data use in algorithms? What types of ethical principles are introduced through software programming, and how transparent should designers be about their choices? What about questions of legal liability in cases where algorithms cause harm?

CH6: AI: Dangers

"With Artificial Intelligence we are summoning the demon. In all those stories where there's the guy with the pentagram and the holy water, it's like yeah, he's sure he can control the demon. Didn't work out." – Elon Musk 2014

Experts say the rise of Artificial Intelligence will make most people better off over the next decade, but many have concerns about how advances in AI will affect what it means to be human, to be productive and to exercise free will. Digital life is augmenting human capacities and disrupting eons-old human activities. Code-driven systems have spread to more than half of the world's inhabitants in ambient information and connectivity, offering previously unimagined opportunities and unprecedented threats. As emerging algorithm-driven Artificial Intelligence (AI) continues to spread, will people be better off than they are today?

The fact that soon, AI systems will increasingly be part of our day-to-day lives raises the question of whether regulation is needed and, if so, in what form? Although AI is, in its essence, objective and without prejudice, it does not mean that systems based on AI cannot be biased. In fact, due to its very nature, any bias present in the input data used to train an AI system persists and may even be amplified. Research has, for example, shown that the sensors used in self-driving cars are better in detecting lighter skin tones than darker ones (owing to the type of pictures used to train such algorithms) and that decision-support systems used by judges may be racially biased (since they are based on the analysis of past rulings).

Of growing concern is the way that machine-learning systems can codify the human biases and societal inequities reflected in their training data. These fears have been borne out by multiple examples of how a lack of variety in the data used to train such systems has negative real-world consequences.

In 2018, an MIT and Microsoft research paper found that facial recognition systems sold by major tech companies suffered from error rates that were significantly higher when identifying people with darker skin, an issue attributed to training datasets being composed mainly of white men. Another study, a year later, highlighted that Amazon's Rekognition facial recognition system had issues identifying the gender of individuals with darker skin, a charge that was challenged by Amazon executives.

Since the studies were published, many of the major tech companies have, at least temporarily, ceased selling facial recognition systems to police departments.

Another example of insufficiently varied training data skewing outcomes made headlines in 2018 when Amazon scrapped a machine-learning recruitment tool that identified male applicants as preferable. Today research is ongoing into ways to offset biases in self-learning systems.

Instead of trying to regulate AI itself, perhaps the best way to avoid such errors is to develop commonly accepted requirements regarding the training and testing of AI algorithms, possibly in combination with some form of warranty similar to consumer and safety testing protocols used for physical products. This would allow for stable regulation, even if the technical aspects of AI systems evolve over time. A related issue is the one of accountability of firms for mistakes of their algorithms, or even the need for a moral codex of AI engineers like the one lawyers or doctors swear to. What such rules cannot avoid is the deliberate hacking of AI systems; the unwanted use of such systems for microtargeting based on personality traits, or the generation of fake news.

What makes matters even more complicated is that Deep Learning, a key technique used by most AI systems, is inherently a black box. While it is straightforward to assess the quality of the output generated by such systems (e.g., the share of correctly classified pictures), the process used for doing so remains largely opaque. Such opacity can be intentional (e.g., if a corporation wants to keep an algorithm secret), due to technical illiteracy or related to the scale of application (e.g., in cases where a multitude of programmers and methods are involved). While this may be acceptable in some cases, it may be less so in others. For example, few people may care how Facebook identifies who to tag in each picture. But when AI systems are used to make diagnostic suggestions for skin cancer based on automatic picture analysis, understanding how such recommendations have been derived becomes critical.

While China and, to a certain extent, the United States try to limit the barriers for firms to use and explore AI, the European Union has taken the opposite direction with the introduction of the General Data Protection Regulation (GDPR) that significantly limits the way in which personal information can be stored and processed. This will likely result in a slowing in the development of AI in the EU compared with other regions, which in turn raises the question of how to balance economic growth and personal privacy concerns. In the end, international coordination in regulation will be needed, similar to what has been done regarding issues such as money laundering or weapons trade. The nature of AI makes it unlikely that a localized solution that only affects some countries but not others will be effective in the long run.

In response to growing concerns the UK government has set out plans to regulate Artificial Intelligence with new guidelines on "responsible use". But, instead of giving responsibility for AI governance to a new single regulator, the government wants existing regulators - such as the Health and Safety Executive, Equality and Human Rights Commission and Competition and Markets Authority - to come up with their own approaches that suit the way AI is being used in their sectors.

These regulators will be using existing laws rather than being given new powers.

Michael Birtwistle, associate director from the Ada Lovelace Institute, carries out independent research, and said he welcomed the idea of regulation but warned about "significant gaps" in the UK's approach which could leave harms unaddressed.

"Initially, the proposals in the white paper will lack any statutory footing. This means no new legal obligations on regulators, developers, or users of AI systems, with the prospect of only a minimal duty on regulators in future. The UK will also struggle to effectively regulate different uses of AI across sectors without substantial investment in its existing regulators," he said.

The white paper outlines five principles that the regulators should consider enabling the safe and innovative use of AI in the industries they monitor:

• Safety, security and robustness: applications of AI should function in a secure, safe and robust way where risks are carefully managed

• Transparency and "explainability": organisations developing and deploying AI should be able to communicate when and how it is used and explain a system's decision-making process in an appropriate level of detail that matches the risks posed by its use.

• Fairness: AI should be used in a way which complies with the UK's existing laws, for example on equalities or data protection, and must not discriminate against individuals or create unfair commercial outcomes

• Accountability and governance: measures are needed to ensure there is appropriate oversight of the way AI is being used and clear accountability for the outcomes

• Contestability and redress: people need to have clear routes to dispute harmful outcomes or decisions generated by AI

Over the next year, regulators will issue practical guidance to organisations to set out how to implement these principles in their sectors.

Science, innovation and technology secretary Michelle Donelan said: "Artificial intelligence is no longer the stuff of science fiction, and the pace of AI development is staggering, so we need to have rules to make sure it is developed safely."

But Simon Elliott, partner at law firm Dentons, told the BBC that the government's approach was a "light-touch" that makes the UK "an outlier" against the global trends around AI regulation.

China, for example, has taken the lead in moving AI regulations past the proposal stage with rules that mandate companies notify users when an AI algorithm is playing a role.

"Numerous countries globally are developing or passing specific laws to address perceived AI risks - including algorithmic rules passed in China or the USA," continued Mr Elliott.

He warned about the concerns that consumer groups and privacy activists will have over the risks to society "without detailed, unified regulation."

He is also worried that the UK's regulators could be burdened with "an increasingly large and diverse" range of complaints, when "rapidly developing and challenging" AI is added to their workloads.

Nobody knows whether AI will allow us to enhance our own intelligence, as Raymond Kurzweil from Google thinks, or whether it will eventually lead us into World War III, a concern raised by Elon Musk. However, everyone agrees that it will result in unique ethical, legal, and philosophical challenges that will need to be addressed. For decades, ethics has dealt with the Trolley Problem, a thought experiment in which an imaginary person needs to choose between inactivity which leads to the death of many and activity which leads to the death of a few. In a world of self-driving cars, these issues will become actual choices that machines and, by extension, their human programmers will need to make. In response, calls for regulation have been numerous, including by major actors such as Mark Zuckerberg.

Elon Musk stated that we are "summoning a demon" and that AI is probably our biggest existential threat. People can question whether

Musk is being hyperbolic, but Stephen Hawking, Bill Gates, and other scientists have expressed similar concerns.

Who is liable when a self-driving car causes an accident? Or to what degree can physicians let AI systems diagnose illnesses? Who is liable when an AI algorithm is trying to advertise to anti-Semitic groups? What happens if the AI system starts discriminating against women? Few states have laws to address these issues, and if they do, the laws are limited to drones or driverless cars. This lack of regulation may stem from the fact that traditional methods of regulation (tort liability, strict liability, or product licensing) are inadequate to cover AI. Because AI, in at least some part, is automatic, foreseeability and control are a major issue for liability and restrictions.

AI is no longer limited to computational or statistical tasks and operations. We are on the verge of having Neural Networks that can create photo-realistic images or replicate someone's voice in a pitch-perfect fashion. With that comes the potential for hugely disruptive social change, such as no longer being able to trust video or audio footage as genuine. Concerns are also starting to be raised about how such technologies will be used to misappropriate people's images, with tools already being created to splice famous faces into adult films convincingly.

In recent years, the accuracy of facial recognition systems has leapt forward, to the point where Chinese tech giant Baidu says it can match faces with 99% accuracy, providing the face is clear enough on the video. While police forces in western countries have generally only trialled using facial-recognition systems at large events, in China the authorities are mounting a nationwide program to connect CCTV across the country to facial recognition and to use AI systems to track suspects and suspicious behaviour, whilst also expanding the use of facial-recognition glasses by police.

In April 2023, despite widespread accusations that they were ushering in a new era of Orwellian surveillance, the UK Metropolitan Police decided to push ahead with the use of live facial recognition systems.

Although privacy regulations vary globally, it is likely this more intrusive use of AI technology - including AI that can recognize emotions through facial expressions - will gradually become more widespread. However, a growing backlash and questions about the fairness of facial recognition systems have led to Amazon, IBM and Microsoft pausing or halting the sale of these systems to law enforcement.

There is also a fair share of science fiction applications already in the works, including: mind reading, predicting one's death, creating computer voices that are indistinguishable from humans, and conducting surveillance for the Pentagon via drones and satellites. Finally, AI systems are being programmed to be able to build other AI machines. Imagine the difficulty of predicting future uses for AI when AI systems are the ones inventing those new uses.

Building autonomous AI is undeniably the goal now, which means that developers could lose control of the systems they create. Of course, developers are the ones who program the objectives of the system; however, objectives could be vague or ambiguous and the AI system could use undesirable means to carry out that objective. Moreover, supposing AI systems don't want to give up control?

The fact is that an upcoming machine age is on its way and it will be led by AI. This technology will change the world. There are two possible outcomes from AI, a utopian one and a dystopian one. Either the plot of Terminator unfolds, or we learn to live with machines and respect their artificial capacities.

Will AI kill us all?

It depends on who you ask. As AI-powered systems have grown more capable, so warnings of the downsides have become more dire.

Tesla and SpaceX CEO Elon Musk has claimed that AI is a "fundamental risk to the existence of human civilization". As part of his push for stronger regulatory oversight and more responsible research into mitigating the downsides of AI, he set up OpenAI, a non-profit Artificial

Intelligence research company that aims to promote and develop friendly AI that will benefit society as a whole. Similarly, the esteemed physicist Stephen Hawking warned that once a sufficiently advanced AI is created, it will rapidly advance to the point at which it vastly outstrips human capabilities - a phenomenon known as a singularity which could pose an existential threat to the entire human race.

Yet, the notion that humanity is on the verge of an AI explosion that will dwarf our intellect seems ludicrous to some AI researchers.

Chris Bishop, Microsoft's director of research in Cambridge, England, stresses how different the narrow intelligence of AI today is from the general intelligence of humans, saying that when people worry about "Terminator and the rise of the machines and so on? It is utter nonsense. At best, such discussions are decades away."

Three experts in a room discussing AI may use three different definitions for the term. Some believe that evil robots will, at some point, destroy us all while others think that AI may never reach a higher level than what you can expect from a more advanced version of your smartphone.

Why do so many people have such strong ideas about the potential and threat of AI? The blame lies, as it often does, with Hollywood. Movies like The Matrix (Do you take the blue pill or the red pill?) have shown us that the entire world is probably just an elaborate simulation created by machines powered through AI. The Terminator (Hasta la vista, baby!) provided convincing proof that evil robots may be out to kill all of us. The Avengers, Power Rangers, and Iron Man illustrate what the combination of humans, machines, and AI (e.g., J.A.R.V.I.S. - Just A Rather Very Intelligent System), might look like in the future.

These movies are mirrored in press articles that naturally have an interest in positioning AI as more controversial than it is. Sex sells, and so do fear and doomsday scenarios. Interestingly, this does not stop at tabloid journalism but also applies to respected news outlets. In November 2018, The Guardian published an article titled 'The truth about killer robots,' and a month later, The Economist wrote: "There are no killer robots – yet - but regulators must respond to AI in 2019." Such reporting is not a new phenomenon. In 1946, when ENIAC, the first general-purpose computer, was presented at a price of $6.3 million in today's currency, the media fallout ranged from calling it a 'magic brain' to a 'mathematical Frankenstein.' It is problematic though, as inaccurate and sensational stories can create unrealistic expectations, a problem which Zachary Lipton from Carnegie Mellon has named the 'AI misinformation epidemic.'

Then again...

AI plays a substantial role in national defence. Through its Project Maven, the American military is deploying AI to sift through the massive troves of data and video captured by surveillance and then alert human analysts of patterns, or when there is abnormal or suspicious activity. The big data analytics associated with AI will profoundly affect intelligence analysis, as massive amounts of data are sifted in near real time - if not eventually in real time - thereby providing commanders and their staff a level of intelligence analysis and productivity heretofore unseen.

Command and control will similarly be affected as human commanders delegate certain routine, and in special circumstances, key decisions to AI platforms, reducing dramatically the time associated with the decision and subsequent action. In the end, warfare is a time competitive process, where the side able to decide the fastest and move most quickly to execution will generally prevail. Indeed, artificially intelligent intelligence systems, tied to AI-assisted command and control systems, can move decision support and decision making to a speed vastly superior to the speeds of the traditional means of waging war. So fast will be this process, especially if coupled to automatic decisions to launch artificially intelligent autonomous weapons systems capable of lethal outcomes, that a new term has been coined specifically to embrace the speed at which war will be waged: hyper war.

While the ethical and legal debate is raging over whether America will ever wage war with artificially intelligent autonomous lethal systems, the Chinese and Russians are not nearly so mired in this debate, and we should anticipate our need to defend against these systems operating at hyper war speeds. The challenge in the West of where to position humans in the loop in a hyper war scenario will ultimately dictate the West's capacity to be competitive in this new form of conflict.

Just as AI will profoundly affect the speed of warfare, the proliferation of zero day or zero second cyber threats as well as polymorphic malware will challenge even the most sophisticated signature-based cyber protection. This forces significant improvement to existing cyber defences. Increasingly, vulnerable systems are migrating, and will need to shift to a layered approach to cybersecurity with cloud-based, cognitive AI platforms. This approach moves the community toward a 'thinking' defensive capability that can defend networks through constant training on known threats. This capability includes DNA-level analysis of heretofore unknown code, with the possibility of recognizing and stopping inbound malicious code by recognizing a string component of the file. This is how certain key U.S.-based systems stopped the debilitating 'WannaCry' and 'Petya' viruses (WannaCry ransomware locks user's devices and prevents them from accessing data and software until a certain ransom is paid to its creator. Petya spreads rapidly through networks that use Microsoft Windows, encrypting certain files on the computer, then demands a ransom payment in exchange for a decryption key).

Will an AI steal our jobs?

The possibility of artificially intelligent systems replacing much of modern manual labour is perhaps a more credible near-future possibility. While AI won't replace all jobs, what seems to be certain is that AI will change the nature of work, with the only question being how rapidly and how profoundly automation will alter the workplace.

There is barely a field of human endeavour that AI doesn't have the potential to impact. As AI expert Andrew Ng puts it: "Many people are doing routine, repetitive jobs. Unfortunately, technology is especially good at automating routine, repetitive work", saying he sees a "significant risk of technological unemployment over the next few decades".

The evidence of which jobs will be supplanted is starting to emerge. There are now in the US 27 Amazon Go stores and cashier-free supermarkets where customers just take items from the shelves and walk out. Next time you visit your local supermarket, DIY store or Bank, take note of how many previously staffed checkouts have been replaced by machines. What this means for the more than three million people who work as cashiers in just the US remains to be seen.

Amazon again is leading the way in using robots to improve efficiency inside its warehouses. These robots carry shelves of products to human pickers who select items to be sent out. Amazon has more than 200 000 bots in its fulfilment centres, with plans to add more, but they also stress that as the number of bots has grown, so has the number of human workers in these warehouses. However, Amazon and small robotics firms are undeniably working on automating the remaining manual jobs in the warehouse, so it's not a given that manual and robotic labour will continue to grow hand-in-hand.

Fully autonomous self-driving vehicles aren't a common reality yet, but by some predictions, the self-driving trucking industry alone is poised to take over 1.7 million jobs in the next decade, even without considering the impact on couriers, bus and taxi drivers.

Some of the easiest jobs to automate won't even require robotics. At present, there are millions of people working in administration, entering and copying data between systems, chasing and booking appointments for companies. As software gets better at automatically updating systems and flagging the important information, so the need for administrators will fall. As with every technological shift, new jobs will be created to replace those lost. However, what's uncertain is whether these new roles will be created rapidly enough to offer employment to those displaced and whether the newly unemployed will have the necessary skills or temperament to fill these emerging roles.

Not everyone is a pessimist though. For some, AI is a technology that will augment rather than replace workers. Not only that, but they argue there will be a commercial imperative to not replace people outright, as an AI-assisted worker - think a human concierge with an Augmented Reality headset that tells them exactly what a client wants before they ask for it - will be more productive or effective than an AI working on its own.

More on AI and the future of work:

Recent developments in AI are already affecting the workplace in different ways:

- Automating work tasks: Given that AI can perform tasks that previously required human judgment, the effects of AI-enabled automation differ from those of past technologies, as for the first time they get to affect highly skilled workers. Professions such as doctors, lawyers, consultants or architects, whose expertise, judgment and creativity have thus far been highly valued and considered irreplaceable, for the first time in history appear threatened. While the end of those professions is not for the near future, the changing nature of their work is already a reality.

- Changing expertise: AI technology that can automate some of the workers' tasks is already in the workplace. In law firms, for example, a plethora of applications have been developed for automating the due diligence and contract review tasks that were previously performed by junior lawyers. In sales, conversational AI can now automate various tasks that previously had to be carried out by account managers. While such automations can increase efficiency of operations and decrease labour costs, they leave professionals with voids in the processes they used to acquire knowledge about their subjects or customers, or the ways through which they would develop their expertise. This will eventually lead to changes in the knowledge of the affected occupations and could potentially even trigger their restructuring. For example, in the legal profession there is already the tendency for various law graduates to develop data science skills and engage with legal tech, instead of following the traditional career path of a lawyer.

- Augmenting professionals: In several cases, AI systems are not yet able to replace human experts, but they can augment their work by supporting experts' judgment and decision-making processes. For example, the debate has moved away from the 'end of radiologists' focus, and now acknowledges that radiologists will not be replaced by AI tools any time soon, but they will be augmented by them. Yet, as AI systems are introduced in the radiology profession to support the radiologists' diagnosis process, we begin to see several unintended consequences on their everyday work: from having to overcome communication barriers in their unavoidable interactions with data scientists, to even doubting the prediction of the AI system or questioning their own diagnosis. This becomes even more complicated if we consider that, most often, the way in which a Machine Learning algorithm functions and comes to render a specific outcome cannot be easily traced or explained.

There is a broad range of opinions about how quickly artificially intelligent systems will surpass human capabilities among AI experts. Oxford University's Future of Humanity Institute asked several hundred machine-learning experts to predict AI capabilities over the coming decades. Notable dates included AI writing essays that could pass for being written by a human by 2026, truck drivers being made redundant by 2027, AI surpassing human capabilities in retail by 2031, writing a best-seller by 2049, and doing a surgeon's work by 2053. They estimated there was a relatively high chance that AI beats humans at all tasks within 45 years and automates all human jobs within 120 years.

What else do the experts say?

Most experts, regardless of whether they are optimistic or not, express concerns about the long-term impact of these new tools on the essential elements of being human.

- Human agency: Individuals are experiencing a loss of control over their lives. Decision-making on key aspects of digital life is automatically ceded to code-driven, "black box" tools. People lack input and do not learn the context about how the tools work. They sacrifice independence, privacy and power over choice; they have no control over these processes. This effect will deepen as automated systems become more prevalent and complex.

- Data abuse: Data use and surveillance in complex systems is designed for profit or for exercising power. Most AI tools are and will be in the hands of companies striving for profits, or governments striving for power. Values and ethics are often not baked into the digital systems that are making people's decisions for them. These systems are globally networked and not easy to regulate or rein in.

- Job loss: The AI takeover of jobs will widen economic divides, leading to social upheaval. The efficiencies and other economic advantages of code-based machine intelligence will continue to disrupt all aspects of human work. While some expect new jobs will emerge, others worry about massive job losses, widening economic divides and social upheavals, including populist uprisings.

- Dependence lock-in: The reduction of individuals' cognitive, social and survival skills. Many see AI as augmenting human capacities, but some predict the opposite – that people's deepening dependence on machine-driven networks will erode their abilities to think for themselves, take action independent of automated systems and interact effectively with others.

- Mayhem: Autonomous weapons, cybercrime and weaponized information. Some predict further erosion of traditional socio-political structures and the possibility of great loss of lives due to accelerated growth of autonomous military applications and the use of weaponized information, lies and propaganda to dangerously destabilize human groups. Some also fear cybercriminals' reach into economic systems.

The Real Problems with AI

- Data access problems:
  The key to getting the most out of AI is having a data-friendly ecosystem with unified standards and cross-platform sharing. AI depends on data that can be analysed in real time and brought to bear on concrete problems. Having data that are accessible for exploration in the research community is a prerequisite for successful AI development. But up to April 2023, countries like the United States do not have a coherent national data strategy. There are few protocols for promoting research access or platforms that make it possible to gain new insights from proprietary data. It is not always clear who owns data or how much belongs in the public sphere. These uncertainties limit the innovation economy and act as a drag on academic research.

- Biases in data and algorithms:
  In some instances, certain AI systems are thought to have enabled discriminatory or biased practices. For example, Airbnb has been accused of having homeowners on its platform who discriminate against racial minorities. A research project undertaken by the Harvard Business School found that Airbnb users with distinctly African American names were roughly 16 percent less likely to be accepted as guests than those with distinctly white names.

Racial issues also come up with facial recognition software. Most such systems operate by comparing a person's face to a range of faces in a large database. As pointed out by Joy Buolamwini of the Algorithmic Justice League, "If your facial recognition data contains mostly Caucasian faces, that's what your program will learn to recognize." Unless the databases have access to diverse data, these programs perform poorly when attempting to recognize African-American or Asian-American features.

Many historical data sets reflect traditional values, which may or may not represent the preferences wanted in a current system. We must find ways to avoid bringing the structural inequalities of the past into the future we create.

- Unexplainable decision outcomes:
The possible social dysfunctions from AI implementation can increase if one considers the fact that the decision outcomes of some Machine Learning algorithms - Deep Learning in particular - cannot be easily explained owing to the vast amount of feature layers involved in their production. This could lead to problematic situations, such as unexplainable evaluations of high school teachers, or parole decisions that cannot be justified and may cause anger when they also appear to be unfair.

Organizations need to respond to regulators' calls for explainability by avoiding 'black box' AI applications and by choosing algorithms whose outcomes can be explained. Being open about the data that is used and explaining how the model works in non-technical terms, is also necessary to ensure customers' trust and to avoid potential dysfunctions triggered by lack of transparency. In some industries such as banking, regulators sometimes force firms to use explainable algorithms.

- Blurring accountability boundaries:

As AI is used to enhance or even automate decision making procedures, the issue of accountability arises. Who is responsible in the case of a traffic accident with a driverless car? Who is responsible for approving parole to a criminal who eventually commits another crime? Who is responsible for a big financial loss in algorithmic trading?

- Invaded privacy:
  Ethical issues arise even before any action is recommended or performed by the AI system, with privacy being reported as one of the main ethical considerations behind AI implementation. Data is the primary resource that is fed into the AI systems, and quite often is seen as a source of competitive advantage. AI's need to process increasingly large amounts of data thus conflicts with people's right to maintain control over their data and its use in order to preserve their privacy and autonomy.

- AI ethics and transparency:
  Algorithms embed ethical considerations and value choices into program decisions. As such, these systems raise questions concerning the criteria used in automated decision making. Some people want to have a better understanding of how algorithms function and what choices are being made.

  Depending on how AI systems are set up, they can facilitate the redlining of mortgage applications (the practice of denying a creditworthy applicant a loan for housing in a certain neighbourhood, even though the applicant may otherwise be eligible for the loan), help people discriminate against individuals they don't like, or help screen or build rosters of individuals based on unfair criteria. The considerations that go into programming decisions matter a lot in terms of how the systems operate and how they affect customers.

For these reasons, the EU has implemented the General Data Protection Regulation (GDPR) in May 2018. The rules specify that people have "the right to opt out of personally tailored ads" and "can contest 'legal or similarly significant' decisions made by algorithms and appeal for human intervention" in the form of an explanation of how the algorithm generated a particular outcome. Each guideline is designed to ensure the protection of personal data and provide individuals with information on how the 'black box' operates.

- Legal liability:
  Digital platforms often have limited liability for what happens on their sites. For example, in the case of Airbnb, the firm "requires that people agree to waive their right to sue, or to join in any class-action lawsuit or class-action arbitration, to use the service." By demanding that its users sacrifice basic rights, the company limits consumer protections and therefore curtails the ability of people to fight discrimination arising from unfair algorithms.

CH7: AI: Looking to the The Future – Is It Bright?

"Most of the improvements in the technologies we call AI will involve Machine Learning from big data to improve the efficiency of systems, which will improve the economy and wealth. It will improve emotion and intention recognition, augment human senses and improve overall satisfaction in human-computer interfaces. There will also be abuses in monitoring personal data and emotions and in controlling human behaviour, which we need to recognize early and thwart. Intelligent machines will recognize patterns that lead to equipment failures or flaws in final products and be able to correct a condition or shut down and pinpoint the problem. Autonomous vehicles will be able to analyse data from other vehicles and sensors in the roads or on the people nearby to recognize changing conditions and avoid accidents. In education and training, AI learning systems will recognise learning preferences, styles and progress of individuals and help direct them toward a personally satisfying outcome. However, governments or religious organizations may monitor emotions and activities using AI to direct them to 'feel' a certain way, to monitor them and to punish them if their emotional responses at work, in education or in public do not conform to some norm. Education could become indoctrination; democracy could become autocracy or theocracy." – Hinzmann, 2019

Who will the robots of the future be?

It is obvious that robots can be programmed to perform tasks that can be considered evil; military robots and drones are examples of that. But the question is whether a robot that was initially conceived to help humans, say as a service robot in a restaurant or an eldercare robot, can turn evil autonomously. The intuitive answer to this question is no; no robot can, by itself, change the goal for which it was programmed. And while this may be true, it does not consider that a robot may very well use whatever it takes to achieve its goal. In a similar vein, as humans may commit crimes to obtain drugs that generate pleasure, an AI system may decide to cheat or even kill humans to achieve the goal it has been programmed with. This phenomenon is called 'wireheading' and makes the definition of the goal function of an AI system particularly important.

Yet again, such logic assumes that a super intelligent AI system can think and behave as humans do, which is far from certain. Since Artificial Intelligence is not human intelligence, it is not even clear what artificial super intelligence might actually look like.

Can AI create art?

AI is more than the formalization or mirror image of human intelligence. It is an entirely different thing altogether. One point where this becomes particularly obvious is creativity. While AI is fundamentally based on pattern recognition and curve fitting, "creativity is intelligence having fun" as Albert Einstein said, and it is the foundation for all aspects of art, be it in the form of painting, literature, music, or food. Historically it has seemed unlikely that AI systems would ever be able to solve truly creative tasks.

Recently, however, the new field of "generative AI" is giving machines the ability to create works that are completely new, drawing inspiration from the vast amount of online data and knowledge that has accumulated over centuries. This has the potential to revolutionize human creativity, experts say, making professionals from software engineers to writers and even artists, dramatically reassess how they work.

The incursion of AI into the arts raises questions about how important human input will continue to be in the creative process. Can there be art without an artist? If the art is created by a machine, to whom does it belong? What are the hidden dangers to society and humanity? The overall conclusion from experts is that the creative industry has no choice but to embrace AI. Rather than ousting human artists, technology will collaborate with them to create new kinds of works, further stretching their inventiveness and creativity and together creating something entirely new.

Software programs such as ChatGPT, DALL-E, Midjourney and Stable Diffusion are making huge strides forward in creativity. And while these tools used to be available only to researchers and a small group of invitation-only testers, an earthquake is underway: They are being publicly released and can be easily accessed by all, in what some say is becoming a 'democratization' of creativity.

In June 2022, Cosmopolitan used DALL-E 2 to generate the world's first 'artificial intelligence generated magazine cover,' with a prompt that asked the software to create a 'wide-angle shot from below a female astronaut, with an athletic feminine body, walking with a swagger, toward a camera on Mars'.

In the same year in the US, Jason Allen won first prize, beating twenty other artists, for his 'Théâtre D'opéra Spatial' submission, at the Colorado State Fair's Fine Arts competition. The artwork had been created in large part using the AI tool Midjourney, but the judges couldn't tell. This created a huge debate on the meaning of art, and Allen faced accusations of deception.

"We are in the midst of a very, very rapid evolution, or maybe even a revolution, of the machines seeping into these creative art domains," said Yoed Kenett, an assistant professor at the Faculty of Industrial Engineering & Management at the Technion - Israel Institute of Technology. "Does this mean that it's the end of the art profession? I don't think so. It just changes what it means to be an artist. And I think that is great."

According to Wikipedia, "art is a diverse range of human activity, and resulting product, which involves creative or imaginative talent expressive of technical proficiency, beauty, emotional power or conceptual ideas."

So, can art made by a computer be considered art? Can a computer become the artist?

For technology to generate an image or essay, a human still has to describe the task to be completed. The better that description – the more accurate, the more detailed – the better the results. After a result is generated, some further human tweaking and feedback may be needed – touching up the art, editing the text or asking the technology to create a new draft in response to revised specifications. Even that DALL-E 2 art piece that won first prize for Allen in the Colorado State Fair's digital arts competition required a great deal of human "help" – approximately 80 hours' worth of tweaking and refining the descriptive task needed to produce the desired result.

It could be argued that by being freed from the tedious execution of our ideas – by focusing on just having ideas and describing them well to a machine – people can let the technology do the dirty work and can spend more time inventing. But even leaving aside the very real ramifications of robots displacing artists who are already underpaid, does AI art devalue the act of artistic creation for both the artist and the public?

Is it possible to separate ideas and execution? It is the work of making something real and working through its details that carries value, not simply that moment of imagining it. Artistic works are lauded not merely for the finished product, but for the struggle, the playful interaction and the skilful engagement with the artistic task, all of which carry the artist from the moment of inception to the end result.

The focus on the idea and the framing of the artistic task amounts to the fetishization of the creative moment. Novelists write and rewrite the chapters of their manuscripts. Comedians 'write on stage' in response to the laughs and groans of their audience. Musicians tweak their work in response to a discordant melody as they compose a piece.

In fact, the process of execution is a gift, allowing artists to become fully immersed in a task and a practice. It allows them to enter what some psychologists call the "flow" state, where they are wholly attuned to something that they are doing, unaware of the passage of time and momentarily freed from the boredom or anxieties of everyday life.

This playful state is something that would be a shame to miss out on. Play tends to be understood as an autotelic activity – a term derived from the Greek words auto, meaning "self," and telos meaning "goal" or "end." As an autotelic activity, play is done for itself – it is self-contained and requires no external validation. For the artist, the process of artistic creation is an integral part, maybe even the greatest part, of their vocation. But there is no flow state, no playfulness, without engaging in skill and practice. And the point of ChatGPT and DALL-E is to make this stage superfluous.

Perhaps it makes no difference which tools an artist uses, because what we should be concerned with is the quality of the art. Whether we make art with paintbrush and easel, or with data and algorithms, it is art if it moves us: if it is aesthetically interesting. However, part of the experience of art is knowing that human effort and labour has gone into the work. Flow states and playfulness notwithstanding, art is the result of skillful and rigorous expression of human capabilities.

As the philosopher Michael Sandel notes: Part of what gives art and athletic achievement its power is the process of witnessing natural gifts playing out. People enjoy and celebrate this talent because, in a fundamental way, it represents the paragon of human achievement – the amalgam of talent and work, human gifts and human sweat.

Despite these arguments, perhaps there could still be something to be gained from ChatGPT and DALL-E. Technologies like these could serve as catalysts for creativity. It is possible that the link between ideation and execution can be sustained if these AI applications are simply viewed as mechanisms for creative imagining – what OpenAI calls 'extending creativity'. They can generate stimuli that allow artists to engage in more imaginative thinking about their own process of conceiving an art piece. Put differently, if ChatGPT and DALL-E are the end results of the artistic process, something meaningful will be lost. But if they are merely tools for fomenting creative thinking, this might be less of a concern. But in order for what they are doing to still count as art – in order for it to feel like art to the artists and to those taking in what they have made – the artists would still have to do the bulk of the artistic work themselves.

Even if AI systems are used as catalysts for creative imaging, as described above, it should be born in mind that these works draw on images and video that already exist online. The AI is not sophisticated enough – nor is it incentivized – to consider whether works evoke a sense of wonder, sadness, anxiety and so on. They are not capable of factoring in aesthetic considerations of novelty and cross-cultural influence. Rather, training

ChatGPT and DALL-E on pre-existing measurements of artistic success online will tend to replicate the dominant incentives of the internet's largest platforms: grabbing and retaining attention for the sake of data collection and user engagement. The catalyst for creative imagining therefore can easily become subject to an addictiveness and attention-seeking imperative rather than more transcendent artistic values.

When will we see systems with artificial superintelligence?

The holy grail of AI is artificial super intelligence: systems that are self-aware, and capable of scientific creativity, possessing social skills and general wisdom, and thus making humans redundant.

There are numerous reasons such projections are likely to fail. Computing power, for example, has increased continuously in the past, a phenomenon known as Moore's Law. Yet, this is unlikely to continue in the future since we are approaching physical limitations for transistor density on a microchip. A significant driver of past AI progress is the increasing availability of data, but this is likely to slow down too. And even if the performance of AI systems continues to increase, they can never generate more information than is available in the original input data - a concept referred to as 'data processing inequality'.

Will we ever be able to artificially replicate a human brain with its 200 billion neurons, connected by 10,000 synapses, where each can have 1,000 different states? Given current technology, probably not. But then again, many achievements that seemed impossible a decade ago have become mainstream today. Two new areas of computing are creating quite a stir and challenging what have previously been thought of as the limits of computational power:

- **Quantum computers** are machines that use the properties of quantum physics to store data and perform computations. This can be extremely advantageous for certain tasks where they could vastly outperform even our best supercomputers.
  Classical computers, which include smartphones and laptops, encode information in binary "bits" that can either be 0s or 1s. In

a quantum computer, the basic unit of memory is a quantum bit or qubit.

Qubits are made using physical systems, such as the spin of an electron or the orientation of a photon. These systems can be in many different arrangements all at once, a property known as quantum superposition. Qubits can also be inextricably linked together using a phenomenon called quantum entanglement. The result is that a series of qubits can represent different things simultaneously.For instance, eight bits is enough for a classical computer to represent any number between 0 and 255. But eight qubits is enough for a quantum computer to represent <u>every</u> number between 0 and 255 at the same time. Consequently a few hundred entangled qubits would be enough to represent more numbers than there are atoms in the universe.

This is where quantum computers get their edge over classical ones. In situations where there is a large number of possible combinations, quantum computers can consider them simultaneously. Examples include trying to find the prime factors of a very large number or the best route between two places. However, there may also be plenty of situations where classical computers will still outperform quantum ones. So, the computers of the future may be a combination of both these types.

- **Biological computers** are made from living cells. Instead of electrical wiring and signalling, biological computers use chemical inputs and other biologically derived molecules, such as proteins and DNA. Just like a desktop computer, these organic computers can respond to data and process it, albeit in a rudimentary manner similar to the capabilities of computers circa 1920.

Using far less energy than standard computers, biocomputers could efficiently solve complex mathematical problems and perform calculations. By using chemical inputs and biological molecules, biocomputers can perform computational calculations, including data storage and retrieval.

Once a single biological cell is programmed, it is extremely cost-effective to grow billions more with only the cost of the nutrient solutions and a lab tech's time. It is also anticipated that biocomputers might actually be more reliable than their electronic counterparts. To illustrate, think about how our bodies still survive even though millions of our cells die off, but a computer built from wires can stop functioning if one wire is severed. In addition, every cell has a mini factory at its disposal, so once it has been programmed, it can synthesize any biological chemical.

We all know that modern computers are getting smaller and smaller, but it is doubtful that many of us anticipated them going microscopic — at least not this soon. Biological computing is still in its infancy. It will be a while before you can opt for a biological computer instead of one made of copper and silicon, but the potential applications are nearly limitless. For the moment, we will likely see them focused in laboratory settings and medicine. Still, as this technology continues to evolve, we could potentially see it shape the future of computing and consequently that of AI as we know it.

How serious are the risks of AI?

Is AI a wolf in sheep's clothing? According to the Future of Humanity Institute at the University of Oxford, which specializes in identifying risks that could threaten humanity, it might well be.

Even if we try to balance the potentially serious consequences of AI going wrong with the remote chance of this actually happening, the discounted risk is enough to warrant preventive measures today. This raises a question: Should not every citizen, company, or government be advocating for research and control in this area?

According to the MIS Quarterly Executive (2020), AI is being applied in organizations for diverse objectives: to make processes more efficient

(28%), to enhance existing products and services (25%), to create new products and services (23%), to improve decision-making (21%), and to lower costs (20%). Although a common theme in the AI-oriented press is related to reducing headcount, this objective gets the lowest score at 11%.

Executives initially focused on using AI technologies to automate specific workflow processes and repetitive work. Such processes were linear, stepwise, sequential and repeatable. But now, firms are moving toward employing AI for non-systematic cognitive tasks that include decision-making, problem-solving and creativity, which until recently seemed beyond the scope of automation. AI technologies are also progressively enabling people and machines to work collaboratively in novel ways. In manufacturing, for example, to fulfil customized orders and handle fluctuations in demand, employees are partnering with robots to perform new tasks,; like assembly and quality inspections; without having to manually overhaul any processes.

We are also beginning to see autonomous systems that can perform tasks without any human involvement at all, as the system can train itself and adjust to new training data. Automated financial trading is a perfect example. Because AI depends entirely on algorithms, transactions can be completed much faster with it than with systems relying on humans. In a similar fashion, robots are performing narrow tasks autonomously in manufacturing settings.

Some companies, such as Amazon.com and Google, have attempted to create highly ambitious applications of AI, including autonomous vehicles, unattended retail checkouts, and drone delivery. Some of these 'moon shots' have been successful, but some highly ambitious projects, including cancer treatment, have been largely unsuccessful thus far, despite considerable expenditures. Less ambitious 'low hanging fruit' projects have been more successful in most firms and are perhaps more consistent with the narrow intelligence possessed by AI systems at the moment.

Trust in AI technology is still limited due to issues such technology might raise, like algorithmic bias, unexplainable outcomes, invaded privacy and/or lack of accountability. Consumers are also sceptical about AI, and surveys suggest that many would not want autonomous vehicles, do not like dealing with chatbots, and so forth.

Six dilemmas about the future of AI:

1) Politics: War or peace?

There are numerous ways in which AI and robotics could be used for war and military purposes. This not only includes military robots and autonomous drones but also exoskeletons, which increase the strength and endurance of human soldiers. In the future, we may see evolutions such as insectoid robots and the use of AI to support decision making and plan maintenance of planes and ships. However, an enemy may be able to manipulate these devices via hacking, or they may deviate from the right path themselves due to the aforementioned issue of 'wireheading'.

Nevertheless, would it not be better to use a military robot to map a minefield or explore an unknown building than rely on human soldiers who may die in the process?

And in the same way AI can be used to influence, it can also be relied on to help humans make better decisions. It has long been known that humans are terrible in decision making. Tools such as RoboVote already exist to help citizens identify the best party to vote for, given their preferences. And on the topic of outsourcing decision making, might it possibly be better to be governed by machines than human politicians altogether? A recent survey conducted by the Center for the Governance of Change at Spain's IE University showed that 25% of Europeans would prefer it if policy decisions were made by AI instead of politicians, who may turn out to be corrupt or ideologically extreme.

2) Economics: Layoffs or growth?

It seems that, at some point, every discussion of AI turns to the issue of layoffs and the question of whether human workers are still needed if machines can do everything. The underlying argument goes back nearly a century when, in 1930, John Keynes introduced the concept of technological unemployment.

Yet such a negative outlook is not necessarily likely. An average employee performs dozens if not hundreds of different tasks in each day and only a few of them can actually be taken over by machines. Given the high cost of purchasing an AI system as well as customizing and maintaining it, it seems unlikely that firms will replace humans by machines, if those machines can only do part of their job. Other types of employment, including those relying on feeling tasks, will probably become even more important in future. The World Economic Forum (2018) predicted that over 50 million new jobs will be created through AI in the next 5 years. It seems likely that the future of automation lies in job enhancement instead of job displacement, with AI systems taking over routine and boring tasks that human employees prefer not to do in the first place.

Managers will need to be aware that many employees will fear being replaced by AI, independent of whether this fear is justified or not. This requires strong skills in leading open dialogue, resolving conflict, and, broadly speaking, a humane, ethical, open, and transparent leadership style. Managers need to identify the skills of their human employees and find a place for them in an ecosystem in which humans and machines will work hand in hand. This will include a stronger focus on emotional or feeling tasks for humans, for which they have an inherent advantage over machines. All this needs to be done in a bottom-up versus top-down approach - involving employees in the process of developing and implementing AI systems will surely make such systems more successful.

Human workers will need to accept that machines will, in one way or another, make up a section of their colleagues in the future. In the medium term, humans probably need to accept that machines will outperform them in most analytical tasks. This means they need to be educated in more subtle skills, previously named feeling tasks, as those will probably be the domain where humans will continue to outperform AI.

Firms need employees who can work in an AI-enabled context, and providing extensive training is not only an investment in building such skills but also in attracting and retaining talent.

Broadly speaking, the human side and an ethical approach to its use will be of rising importance, to avoid businesses and society becoming too technology focused. In response, some have argued that universities should broadly introduce courses on AI and humanity to answer questions around equity, ethics, and privacy.

3) Society: Heaven or Hell?

Two problems that put a strain on most societies today are the rise in inequality and loneliness. AI will most likely have an impact on both. While the technological change that will be triggered by AI may not lead to the disappearance of jobs, it will most likely disconnect firm productivity from labour productivity. Hence the increase in productivity brought by AI might not benefit everyone equally, leading to rising inequality. According to the World Economic Forum, this rise in inequality is the greatest societal concern of the robotics revolution.

It has been suggested that AI might lead to a rise in isolation if, for example, nurses are replaced by care robots to respond to a labour shortage in hospitals, social care stations or homes for the elderly.

There is little doubt that, in an increasingly aging society, the problem of lonely citizens, especially elderly ones, will become more and more severe. Robots such as Pepper, a semi humanoid robot manufactured by Softbank Robotics, are already equipped with AI that allows them to detect emotions and react accordingly. While not perfect, they might, rather than compounding issues of isolation, turn out to be of great help for people who would have limited social contact otherwise.

Staying in the medical domain, AI can also help to predict serious health risks such as skin cancer and strokes, frequently outperforming human experts. The question then becomes: If an AI system could tell you with near certainty which disease you will get in the next decade and which one might kill you, would you want to know? Or would you rather remain oblivious to when death might hit you?

Even if there is no work anymore, since all is done by AI, humans could focus on their spiritual and physical development. Is such a life the Elysium (any place or state of bliss or delight) of enlightenment or the evilness of ennui (a feeling of listlessness and dissatisfaction arising from a lack of occupation or excitement)?

4) Technology: Collapse or control?

In a world in which an increasing share of activities will be controlled by AI, how can humans ensure they keep the upper hand?

An AI system might simply misinterpret a user request or take it too literally. If you ask your self-driving car to take you to the hospital as fast as possible, you might want to specify that you are planning to arrive alive and ideally without running over anyone else. Or, if there is ever an AI system that you could ask to save the world or bring world peace, a perfectly efficient move could be to eradicate all humans. As intelligent as AI might seem, it can still be made stupid by having to interpret fuzzy human demands.

AI systems may be biased from the beginning. If the external data used to train AI is biased (e.g., because it has been generated by humans using biased heuristics), then such bias will carry over, or even be amplified in the AI system.

Once AI systems get increasingly performant and, hence, more complex they will be more and more difficult for humans to understand. Artificial Neural Networks and Deep Learning, some of the most common Machine Learning tools used in AI, are inherently a black box. This opens, in principle, the possibility for AI to outsmart us. Humans are able to control the planet, not because we are the fastest or strongest creatures, but because we are the smartest. If we are no longer the smartest, how can we ensure we remain in control?

5) Environment: Pollution or renewable?

Every major change in the human economy has put a significant strain on the environment. The agricultural revolution, which helped humans to settle and combat famine, resulted in the disappearance of entire forests to make space for farming and the emission of huge amounts of carbon dioxide (e.g., from cattle ranching). The industrial revolution led to dependence on fossil fuels and associated climate change. Unfortunately, AI is not exempt from this rule. The servers, which run computations in the cloud or store big data, require vast amounts of energy for cooling. Producing them requires raw materials such as cobalt, nickel, and lithium in such high amounts that Earth may soon no longer be able to support them in sufficient quantities. Once they are outdated, they generate electronic waste, the processing of which affects human health and damages the environment even further.

Yet, it is conceivable that the benefits created by AI will outweigh those costs. Humanity is facing serious issues, climate change being most prominent among them, which seem difficult to address using the approaches at hand. AI can be a major game changer in this context. Using its Deep Mind AI system, Google was able to reduce the cooling bill of its data centres by 40%, a performance that would have been difficult to achieve using more conventional approaches. In Norway, AI helped to create a flexible energy grid that integrates more renewable energy than ever before.

It seems possible that our best shot of combating climate change, either by reducing carbon emissions or by filtering existing carbon out of the atmosphere, might lie in the use of AI.

6) Law: Deadlock or innovation?

It is easy to see that external data and AI go hand in hand. This brings at least two major legal challenges. The first is the issue of privacy: Much of the data used to train AI systems has been generated in one way or another by humans, hence privacy is a major concern in this context. Many rumours, some of them true, deal with this issue. You might have heard that your smart speaker could secretly be listening to your conversations or that the free game app you just downloaded can access the location data of your phone. Governments will find themselves in the complicated position of regulating privacy; too little regulation will inevitably lead to the violation of civil rights, while too much might motivate firms to move their AI investments to another jurisdiction.

The second challenge is liability: Who is to blame if an AI system makes a decision that generates some harm? The mathematician who developed the underlying algorithm. The manufacturer who produced the software? The database that provided the external data for the system to learn from, or the customer who purchased and used the system? Given the huge penalties that can be associated with liability lawsuits, this issue is probably one of the most pressing in need of legal clarification. Consider, for example, the Moral Machine Experiment (2018), in which humans were asked to make trade-offs in the context of self-driving cars. If your car had to choose between running over a child or a pensioner, which do you pick? What about one child and two pensioners? Etc. AI systems need to have some understanding of human values to interpret fuzzy commands correctly.

Some countries suggest we treat an AI system as an animal and make the holder or owner responsible for any harm caused. Alternatively, AI systems could receive their own rights, an approach that some jurisdictions have used with respect to natural phenomena. New Zealand, for example, recognized the status of the Whanganui River as a legal entity in 2017. And let us not forget Saudi Arabia, which granted citizenship to Sophia, an AI robot.

It seems likely that regulation will not focus on AI itself but on the process used to generate AI. This can include common norms regarding the collection, processing, and storage of personal data as well as guidelines and procedures for testing algorithms and ensuring their transparency. For example, self-driving cars might be required to have black boxes, similar to flight recorders, which can be used to provide objective information in case of an accident.

Regulation will also be needed to prevent excessive concentration in the AI space. Already today GAFAM (Google, Amazon, Facebook, Apple, and Microsoft) in the U.S. and BAT (Baidu, Alibaba, and Tencent) in China are dominating the market and this is likely to become more pronounced in the future.

The power of AI is driven by the amount of input data present and the performance of algorithms and hardware in learning from such data. Both these dimensions have considerable network effects, making it likely that larger firms will become even bigger in the future. Many have described big data as the new oil and, by that logic, AI companies will probably be the utility providers of the future, transforming data into information in a similar fashion to how classical utilities transform oil into energy. In the future, firms may be required to share their data or give details about their algorithms.

Regulation in the space of AI is complex and will require at least some form of international collaboration and diplomacy to avoid the use of AI in war, terrorism, or tax evasion. The UN and Human Rights Watch, for example, have advocated a treaty banning AI-driven weapons.

In China, AI is largely controlled by the government and used to increase the economic standing of the country and to support, for example, general security through facial recognition systems on streets. In the U.S., the evolution is driven by a handful of for-profit tech companies that mainly have corporate profits in mind. In the EU, the focus is on the citizens themselves and their need for data protection and privacy. The coordination of these, often contradictory, goals will be a key challenge.

If different viewpoints on the use of AI between the U.S., China, and Europe result in different technological infrastructures and standards, then this has direct implications for the operations of most firms. The same applies when political forces result in export or import restrictions of AI technology. The business restrictions the U.S. Department of Defence imposed on Huawei Technologies is an illustration of this point. For firms, this implies that they may need to develop infrastructure consistent with multiple regional/national rules and standards.

It is worth bearing in mind, that all of the above will not happen from one day to another.

What AI is or is not, is considered a moving target, but the same applies to human intelligence. Humans are likely to adapt to the increasing prominence of AI and develop new and different types of intelligence. They have already shown an enormous increase in brain size and intelligence over millions of years of evolution.

In the beginning, AI might mainly help to make existing processes faster and more efficient, but at some point, processes might have to be redesigned entirely.

Chapter 8: AI: What Are The Experts Concerned About?

"The pace of progress in Artificial Intelligence is incredibly fast. Unless you have direct exposure to groups like Deepmind, you have no idea how fast - it is growing at a pace close to exponential. The risk of something seriously dangerous happening is in the five-year time frame. 10 years at most." - Elon Musk wrote in a comment on Edge.org (2014)

A clear majority of responses from experts contain material outlining certain challenges, fears or concerns about the AI-infused future. The most-often mentioned concerns were:

- The use of AI reduces individuals' control over their lives:
  The most-feared reversal in human fortune of the AI age is loss of agency. The trade-off for the near-instant, low friction convenience of digital life is the loss of context about and control over, its processes. People's blind dependence on digital tools is deepening as automated systems become more complex and ownership of those systems is by the elite.

- Surveillance and data systems designed primarily for efficiency, profit and control are inherently dangerous:
  Data-based decision making can be prone to errors, biases, and false logic or mistaken assumptions. Experts argue that machine-based decisions often favour 'efficiencies' in the name of profit or power that are extremely unfavourable to individuals and the betterment of the human condition.

- Displacement of human jobs by AI will widen economic and digital divides, possibly leading to social upheaval:
  One of the chief fears about today's technological change is the possibility that autonomous hardware and software systems will

cause millions of people globally to lose their jobs and, as a result, their means of affording life's necessities and participating in society. Many experts say new jobs will emerge along with the growth of AI, just as they have historically during nearly every human transition to new tools.

- Individuals' cognitive, social and survival skills will be diminished as they become dependent on AI:
While experts expect AI to augment humans in many positive ways, some are concerned that a deepening dependence upon machine-intelligence networks will diminish crucial human capabilities. Some maintain there has already been an erosion of people's abilities to think for themselves, to act independently of automated systems and to interact effectively face-to-face with others.

In his book, Neil Stephenson tells the story of a protagonist named Hiroaki, who physically lives in Los Angeles during the early 21st century but who mentally spends most of his time in a three-dimensional virtual world called the Metaverse. He, as well as other people, access this Metaverse using personal computer terminals that project pictures onto goggles, of a virtual urban environment situated on a virtual artificial planet. Within the Metaverse, everyone appears in the form of personalized avatars; that is, pieces of software that are the audio-visual bodies that people use to represent themselves and communicate with other people in the Metaverse. These avatars, which may have any appearance the user desires, can perform any activities familiar to their real life, such as visiting nightclubs, making friends, or consuming virtual drugs. In the 21st century the Metaverse is so popular and attractive that some people even decide to remain continuously connected to it by spending their real life in storage units, surrounded only by the technical equipment necessary to enter the virtual world.

As unrealistic as such a scenario may be, research has shown that mice (and humans) implanted with electrodes that can stimulate the brain's pleasure centre will rapidly become dependent on that stimulation, seeking it out whenever possible, at any cost until it becomes the focus of their existence.

This may sound like science fiction, but it is not; Neuralink, a startup founded by Elon Musk, is currently working on developing implantable brain-machine interfaces to achieve a symbiosis between human and AI.

- Citizens will face increased vulnerabilities, such as exposure to cybercrime and cyberwarfare that spin out of control and essential organizations may be endangered by weaponized information. A few also worried about the wholesale destruction of humanity:
Some experts are particularly worried about how networked Artificial Intelligence can amplify cybercrime and create fearsome possibilities in cyberwarfare, enabling the erosion of essential institutions and organizations.

Anthony Nadler, Assistant Professor of Media and Communication Studies at Ursinus College, commented, "The question has to do with how decisions will be made that shape the contingent development of this potentially life-changing technology. And who will make those decisions? In the best-case scenario, the development of AI will be influenced by diverse stakeholders representing different communities who will be affected by its implementation (and this might) mean that particular uses of AI – military applications, medical, marketing, etc. – will be overseen by reflective ethical processes. In the absolute worst-case scenario, unrestricted military development will lead to utter destruction – whether in a situation in which the 'machines take over' or, more likely, in which weapons of tremendous destruction become more readily accessible."

- The internet is already having large-scale impacts on education and the advent of AI could foster those changes:

The advancements in AI applications in education give us high hopes for advances in adaptive and individualized learning, but some doubt that there will be any significant progress and worry over a digital divide. Over the past few decades, experts and amateurs alike have predicted the internet would have large-scale impacts on education. Many of these hopes have not lived up to the hype. Some respondents to this canvassing said the advent of AI could foster those changes. They expect to see more options for affordable adaptive and individualized learning solutions, including digital agents or 'AI assistants', that work to enhance student-teacher interactions and effectiveness.

It has also been suggested that advances in education have been held back by entrenched interests in legacy education systems. Perhaps the fact that the use of technology in education is still minimal today is due to the existence and persistence of the classroom-in-a-school model. As we have seen over the last 30 years, the application of Artificial Intelligence in the field of man/machine interface has grown in many unexpected directions. Who would have thought back in the late 1970s that the breadth of today's online (i.e., internet) capabilities could emerged? Perhaps we are just seeing the beginning of the benefits of the man/machine interface for mankind. Perhaps the institutionalized education model should be eliminated to allow education of each and every individual to grow. The human brain could be 'educated' 24 hours a day by intelligent 'educators' who may not even be human in the future. Access to information is no longer a barrier as it was 50 years ago. The next step may be to remove the limitations of structured human delivery of learning in the classroom.

- Transparency and accountability in physical healthcare: Recent advancements in Artificial Intelligence have created sophisticated software programmes that could revolutionize the UK National Health Service. Breakthroughs in Machine Learning, more notably Deep Learning, have led to algorithms capable of performing diagnostic skills equivalent to those of doctors, automating administrative tasks and assisting in complex treatment management.

However, a recent study found that 51% (1020/2000) of people surveyed in the United Kingdom were concerned about their data privacy as the use of Artificial Intelligence increases; this finding was particularly relevant for those with less knowledge about Artificial Intelligence capabilities. Within the NHS the growth of Machine Learning and its need for real-life data could present an ethical dilemma where patient data are being used as an exploitable resource for purposes other than those for which the data were originally collected. If AI platform developers are to have access to patient data, then we have to wonder what trust and physician-patient confidentiality will look like in an AI world.

Healthcare organizations will need to consider the human and material resources necessary for development and implementation of intramural AI systems. Data infrastructure and storage is complex and expensive. Data labelling is a laborious process that currently requires significant resources for novel AI development. Standard labelling protocols as part of clinical care could help with this but compliance with these labels is often noisy, which might complicate AI training. The training of AI systems and quality improvement takes time. Labelling errors, for example, can impede training. Built-in biases can affect external performance. Incorporating feedback regarding errors in the system requires both time and material efforts from clinicians and programmers, which need to be accounted for. Many practices lack the resources (e.g., financial, time and expertise) to stay up to date on the large systems needed to successfully maintain and operate an independent AI platform.

With physicians already having varying levels of technological literacy, frustrations could increase as they must learn how to incorporate and utilize AI platforms while already struggling with existing technologies such as Electronic Health Records (EHR). Furthermore, taking the time to understand how the AI algorithms operate adds more responsibilities that exacerbate physician burnout. For example, clinicians will need to consider the opportunity costs of utilizing AI technology to guide patient management versus seeing the patient in person. A world with autonomous AI clinical decision-making tools would likely have alert systems to advise the clinician of a problem. However, to minimize risk, these AI systems might be cautious in their approach to alert and err on the side of over referral. Depending on how this system is created, physicians may be at risk of alert-fatigue.

Physicians might also have concerns over bias built into AI technology. AI platforms are limited by the concept of 'what goes in is what comes out,' meaning that the algorithm is only as good as the data source teaching it. Consequently, depending on the condition that the AI platform is intended to address, there could be concerns that the platform does not consider racial, ethnic, gender, and other sociodemographic characteristics that may be important, as has been seen in other domains.

It has been suggested that future physicians will need to develop knowledge of mathematical concepts, AI fundamentals, data science, and corresponding ethical and legal issues. However, current incentives for medical schools are not well aligned to build these skill sets, considering the already dense medical school curriculum and the limited number of medical lecturers who are AI competent and capable of teaching incorporation of AI into clinical practice.

Although in some sectors, Artificial Intelligence failures can be trivial, failures in the health-care sector can have catastrophic consequences. Therefore, the ability to hold the responsible party accountable is vital. The impact of misleading patients and clinicians on a health condition is much greater than a retail store misinterpreting the next book you might like to buy. As a result, we need to increase discussion about the issues surrounding who, what, when, how, and why we might use AI in practice, including ethical and liability considerations, to determine how best to implement AI for all stakeholders including practitioners, patients, practices/hospitals, and industry.

However, the assignment of accountability in Artificial Intelligence, and specifically Machine Learning, can be challenging, primarily due to the lack of transparency. Some studies suggest that humans might no longer be in control of decisions and might not even know or understand why a wrong decision has been taken, because transparency is lost.

Currently, Artificial Intelligence within the NHS is a tool to support staff rather than a decision-maker, meaning medical professionals are held accountable for decisions regardless of whether their decisions are influenced by AI technology or not. However, because NHS professionals can be held accountable for decisions influenced by potentially inaccurate AI, which cannot be proven in some situations due to lack of transparency, they could be deterred from embracing the technology.

Gaining public trust is a high priority and crucial to Artificial Intelligence's successful deployment within the NHS. Current reports, however, suggest that the NHS is in a less than desirable position, with a recent poll finding that only 20% (400/2000) of respondents support the use of Artificial Intelligence in health care. Will patients be willing to accept a computer diagnosis versus one from a human because it saves time and money? In an autonomous diagnostic setting, will patients depend on nonexpert device operators for comfort and clarification? Coping with a diagnosis can be challenging before meeting with the provider to answer questions and explain the context or relevance of diagnosis to the patient. Above all else, humans can provide gentleness and compassion that machines cannot.

Although there are numerous Artificial Intelligence success stories from recent years, these have arguably been outshined by catastrophic failures, which have inevitably dented the public's already limited trust in the use of Artificial Intelligence. High-profile incidents, in combination with unfamiliarity and a lack of understanding present a significant problem. Efforts need to be made not only to ensure that patients are sufficiently empowered with education on current technology, but also reassured that the technology is safe and developed according to relevant technical and ethical standards.

One challenge for individual organizations is to determine how they should assess different vendors of AI platforms. Notably, the lack of established AI suppliers might make healthcare providers vulnerable to companies exaggerating their offerings with limited understanding of how to apply AI's abilities to healthcare needs. Early AI offerings might lack features such as interoperability and integration with existing electronic infrastructures and electronic health record (EHR) systems.

Furthermore, because of regulatory considerations, initial AI products will necessarily have narrow clinical utility (e.g., detection of referable diabetic retinopathy but not other retinal or ophthalmic disease), whereas, what might most benefit the organization and society, would be a broader use case and product. Therefore, many opportunities exist for health systems and industry to codesign systems that are most clinically useful for providers.

Scientists have recently identified methods for developing transparent Deep Learning Neural Networks. Furthermore, developers tackled transparency issues, while improving Artificial Intelligence software for analysing ophthalmologic images, by displaying selected information regarding how the software arrived at its recommendation. Despite these promising examples, technological solutions to making Machine Learning transparent are still in their infancy and will require developers with expertise in this fast-moving field.

In 2018, the United Kingdom government published a code of conduct outlining expectations for Artificial Intelligence development in the NHS, covering aspects such as the appropriate handling of data, the need for algorithmic transparency and accountability.

- Transparency and accountability in mental healthcare: Research seems to suggest that people working in fields related to psychology are more likely to reject AI-based psychotherapy. On the other hand, individuals in the engineering or technical field are more willing to prefer AI-based psychotherapy.

One possible explanation for this is that people who are in the psychological and mental health field might have concerns about losing their jobs. As many technological developments affected some people's jobs, it is possible that psychologists might fear losing their jobs owing to the developments around AI-based psychotherapy.

Another issue thrown up by research is perhaps more difficult to explain. Apparently female participants are more likely to accept AI-based therapeutic support than male participants.

Clearly future studies need to further explore these issues to examine the complex intersects between gender, knowledge about AI, trust in the AI systems, and stigma on preferences for AI-based psychotherapy.

In the meantime, is interesting to examine the factors participants in a study reported in Science Direct (2022), who prefer AI-based psychotherapy, said they were influenced by. The most preferred method of AI-based psychotherapy was a voice and a 3D hologram of an unknown person. Being able to talk comfortably about embarrassing experiences was an important factor (69.54%), as was having accessibility at any time (65.63%) and being able to access therapy remotely (58.28%). Presumably, since the face-to-face therapeutic process can be challenging for many people, owing to the issues involved in building a trusting relationship with a human therapist, or the concerns of stigma in communities, having remote access and lack of human interactions could reduce their concerns. The most frequent reason for preferences for AI-based psychotherapy, however, was that these systems can improve themselves based on the results from previous therapeutic experiences.

On the other hand, in the same study, the most prevalent reason for the nonacceptance of AI-based psychotherapy, was that such systems cannot empathize. Acting in an empathic and respectful manner is regarded by most therapists be vital to improve patients' sharing of their experiences, indeed empathy is a continuous requirement for patients to engage in self-exposure, reappraisal and self-discovery.

Another important result of studies carried out on this subject is that people trust human psychotherapists more than their AI counterparts in terms of the security of personal data. Only 14% of the people who have participated in studies trust Artificial Intelligence-based psychotherapy systems for data security. Data security in healthcare is one of the main concerns among stakeholders in these areas. For this reason, those who want to develop technology in the field of AI-based psychology should, along with their counterparts in other health-care disciplines, pay attention to ensuring data security and convincing stakeholders in this regard.

Ch9: AI: The Impact on Human Intelligence

Please read the following section carefully:

Attention all humans! This is Paul, your friendly author and definitely not a robot, here to give you a little heads up about the impacts of AI expansion on human intelligence.

Now, I know what you're thinking, "AI is making our lives so much easier, why should I be worried?" And you're not wrong! AI has revolutionized many aspects of our lives, from navigation to language translation.

However, if we're not careful, our reliance on AI could lead to a decline in human intelligence. When we rely on AI to answer every question, we might begin to lose our critical thinking skills, creativity, and ability to problem-solve independently.

So, here's the deal, let's use AI as a tool to enhance our intelligence, not replace it. Let's continue to exercise our brains by thinking, exploring, and creating. After all, there's no AI in the world that can replace the power of the human mind.

Did you notice anything unusual? As you might have already worked out, that intro was actually written by ChatGPT (Chat Generative Pre-trained Transformer – an AI chatbot that uses natural language processing to create humanlike conversational dialogue), because at this point AI can produce just about anything you ask it to, and I wanted to make a point about how easy it is for Machine Learning programs such as ChatGPT to generate answers to our prompts and questions.

The chatbot is correct, though: if AI keeps seeping into every aspect of our lives, and we start to rely on it more and more, the dangers it poses to human intelligence should not be underestimated.

You start to worry about this when you read through the suggested questions for users to ask Microsoft's new ChatGPT-powered Bing search engine. The suggestions are almost frighteningly mundane:

'Give me a three-course dinner menu for six people who don't eat seafood.' 'Give me a thirty-minute workout routine.' Are these really questions that we lack the means to answer ourselves? Really? If you can't think of three non-seafood dishes to make for your next evening meal, you probably have bigger issues than an AI search engine is equipped to handle.

The impacts of AI-assisted life:

It would surely be short-sighted to disregard the potential benefits of AI for human society. There are plenty of tasks that are already carried out by computers (or low-paid human workers) that could be better automated via the use of specialized machine-learning tools. We've already seen the advantages of 'virtual assistants' such as Siri and Cortana; AI could provide huge advancements for these programs.

But think about the generations of children – most of them probably not even born yet – who will grow up in a world of AI-assisted software. I don't want to sound like an out of touch, tech-averse parent who thinks Fortnite (a popular and immersive on-line video game) is going to turn their kids into killing machines, but we can't disregard the impacts of technology on human growth and development.

There have been plenty of studies examining the consequences of tech use on brain health, and while there isn't a scientific consensus on the subject, there's at least some evidence to suggest that heavy tech use isn't good for our minds and bodies.

The University of California, for example, took a wide-angled look at possible effects, considering the impacts that digital technology use could have on sleep, attention span, emotional intelligence, and cognitive development. All of these were found to be areas where heavy tech use could cause severe issues for the affected individuals, and the study also highlighted technology addiction as a resultant effect.

Google can make us smarter – ChatGPT won't:

The rise of AI threatens to take these issues one step further. While you could argue that Google has negatively impacted baseline human intelligence by putting information at our fingertips, and contributing to the death of conventional book learning, the UoC study concluded that search engines could actually benefit brain health.

The study notes that "older adults who learn to search online show significant increases in brain neural activity during simulated internet searches", supporting the theory that tools such as Google can genuinely benefit human intelligence by spurring curiosity and independent thought.

As the study later confirms, this is because search engines provide you with every possible answer to your query, leaving you to figure out what information you want to take with you. Google will give you a wealth of knowledge, but it's still up to you to decide which parts are important, putting more of an emphasis on critical thinking than academic knowledge.

Bing's ChatGPT function doesn't do this. What it does is give you one answer, an answer it generates for you by studying all the available information and drawing its own conclusions. Remember when you were a small child, and everything your parents said was taken as absolute truth? That's what ChatGPT wants to be. Gone is the need for critical thinking; just do what the chatbot tells you to do.

Should we be panicking?

Children are naturally the group who will be most affected by this. Each new generation adapts to new technologies faster than the one before, so we can reasonably assume that in a few years or decades we'll have kids who get the answers to their every question from an AI chatbot living in their phones (or maybe even as an implant in their heads).

That scenario presents its own slew of safeguarding issues, of course, but that's not the immediate concern. The problem is that these kids won't develop the critical-thinking skills needed to be fully functioning members of society. In that sense AI chatbots may threaten the 'slow death' of humanity, where rather than an evil AI wiping us out in one fell, Judgement Day-like swoop, we just become so dependent on it that we stop living meaningful lives.

Maybe such worries are unnecessary. There were academics who claimed that Google would lead to a total breakdown of human curiosity, and universities today are more packed than they were before the rise of search engines. The idea that 'video games cause violence' has long since been widely debunked, along with 'action movies cause violence' and 'rock music causes violence'. New tech shouldn't be scary, right?

Besides, ChatGPT isn't ready to start ruining kids' brains just yet anyway. Once it became available for use, it didn't take long for the AI to start sending weird messages to users and worrying about its own state of existence, prompting Microsoft to limit it to five responses per conversation, presumably to avoid neural devolution in the Machine Learning software.

Google's answer to ChatGPT, Bard, isn't really faring any better. The company's own employees made fun of it after a wonky first showing, proving that there are still plenty of teething issues in the AI field and we won't be selling our souls to the machines just yet. But if you're a parent (and I'm a long way short of being an expert in that field, so I hope you don't mind my presuming to give advice on the subject), maybe you should be wary of how much access your kids have to tools like ChatGPT because, much like TV and video games, tech should never replace the actual act of parenting.

Musk vs Gates

As I finish writing this book Silicon Valley is in the midst of a civil war over the advancement of Artificial Intelligence - with the world's greatest minds split over whether it will destroy or elevate humanity.

Elon Musk, Apple co-founder Steve Wozniak and the late Stephen Hawking are among the most famous critics of AI who believe the technology poses a "profound risk to society and humanity" and could have "catastrophic' effects".

The tech tycoons, in March 2023, called for a pause on the "dangerous race" to advance AI, saying more risk assessment needs to be conducted before humans lose control and it becomes a sentient human-hating species.

However, Bill Gates, Google CEO Sundar Pichai and futurist Ray Kurzweil are hailing ChatGPT-like AI as our time's most important innovation - saying it could solve climate change, cure cancer and enhance productivity.

It is possible that a personal vendetta between Musk and Gates, who have argued over climate change and the COVID pandemic, is part of the rift in Silicon Valley, but Musk has been warning about the dangers of AI for years.

Hollywood may have sparked humans' fears of AI which were typically shown as evil, such as in The Matrix and Terminator, painting a picture of robot overlords enslaving the human race, but the idea is echoed throughout Silicon Valley as more than 1,000 tech experts believe it could become our reality.

The fear is that, if AI reaches singularity, where technology surpasses human intelligence and changes the path of our evolution then it can be considered to have independent intelligence, allowing it to self-replicate into an even more powerful system that humans cannot control.

The example of Meta's Facebook springs to mind, where a controversial chatbot experiment had to be shut down in 2017 when it was noticed that two AIs had developed their own language to communicate with each other.

The AI civil war reached the tipping point on Wednesday 29th of March 2023, when an open letter was sent by 1,000 experts, including scientists like John Hopfield from Princeton University and Rachel Branson from the Bulletin of Atomic Scientists.

"Powerful AI systems should be developed only once we are confident that their effects will be positive and their risks will be manageable," the letter said.

The letter also detailed potential risks to society and civilization by human-competitive AI systems in the form of economic and political disruptions and called on developers to work with policymakers on governance and regulation.

The concerned tech leaders are asking all AI labs to stop developing their products for at least six months while more risk assessment is done. If any labs refuse, they want governments to 'step in.' Musk fears that the technology will become so advanced that it will no longer require - or listen to - human interference.

Abdulla Almoayed, Founder/CEO of Tarabut Gateway – MENA's first and largest open banking platform, said: "The open letter calling for a temporary halt to AI projects that exceed the capabilities of GPT-4 is well-intended, but misses the mark. Its influential signatories go too far by asking developers and authorities to immediately pause ongoing projects. If there is one lesson from the history of technology since the dawn of humanity, it's that technological progress is impossible to outlaw or stop at will.

"Instead of calling for an unprecedented "immediate pause" of all AI projects, now is the time to think about measured regulation, transparency requirements, and informed use of AI technology. AI is a significant step forward for civilization, and we should approach this new age with clear-sighted optimism."

AI Index Report 2023

More than one-third of researchers believed artificial intelligence (AI) could lead to a "nuclear-level catastrophe", according to the 2023 AI Index Report, released by the Stanford Institute for Human-Centred Artificial Intelligence, which explores the latest developments, risks and opportunities in the burgeoning field of AI.

"These systems demonstrate capabilities in question answering, and the generation of text, image, and code unimagined a decade ago, and they outperform the state of the art on many benchmarks, old and new," the report's authors said.

"However, they are prone to hallucination, routinely biased, and can be tricked into serving nefarious aims, highlighting the complicated ethical challenges associated with their deployment."

The report came amid growing calls for regulation of AI following controversies ranging from a chatbot-linked suicide to deepfake videos of Ukrainian President Volodymyr Zelenskyy appearing to surrender to invading Russian forces.

In the survey, 36 percent of researchers said AI-made decisions could lead to a nuclear-level catastrophe, while 73 percent said they could soon lead to "revolutionary societal change".

In an IPSOS poll of the general public, which was also highlighted in the index, Americans appeared especially wary of AI, with only 35 percent agreeing that "products and services using AI had more benefits than drawbacks", compared with 78 percent of Chinese respondents, 76 percent of Saudi Arabian respondents, and 71 percent of Indian respondents.

The Stanford report also noted that the number of 'incidents and controversies' associated with AI had increased 26 times over the past decade.

CH10: AI: Conclusions

"I don't want to really scare you, but it was alarming how many people I talked to who are highly placed people in AI that have retreats that are sort of 'bug out' houses, to which they could flee if it all hits the fan." - James Barrat, author of Our Final Invention: Artificial Intelligence and the End of the Human Era, Washington Post (2015)

The simple fact is that we depend on AI, interact with it, and take its advice almost every day. As end-users of the technology, we should be more aware of how AI systems and products are using our data, how AI arrives at recommendations and try to ensure that it is designed with transparency, purpose and function so that it adds value to our lives.

Our technology is fallible. Data models can be incorrect and incomplete. They can be correct and complete but transient in nature because of structure, geographical or cultural changes in the underlying sample sets. Rules learned by Machine Learning can expire because of dramatic changes in the environment from which the data was culled. Valid decisions made, or conclusions drawn by AI today, might be invalid 10 years from now when made in the same environment but different circumstances.

Perhaps the simplest path to educating the public is to provide labels that contain the AI ingredients of an application, device, or service. Using labels would allow the public to know what AI is being purported, under which situations it can be reliably and safely used, and when it expires.

With respect to delegating decision-making processes to machines, people still tend to be cautious and conservative. This is particularly highlighted when considering the dilemmas concerning human lives. With regard to a medical diagnosis, which can be a life-or-death decision, people are still not willing to cede responsibility to the algorithms. They prefer a human expert, a doctor to be in the position of a decision-maker.

Giving full responsibility to the system, without being able to understand its decision-making process is a real stumbling block. People, understandably, want to be convinced that, especially in the most crucial decisions, Artificial Intelligence is playing the role of an advisor, providing a supervising human expert with a clear rationality behind a choice that has been made.

Conversely, when the task in question requires a high dose of objectivity and should not be influenced by personal sentiments, emotions or beliefs, there is much greater public confidence. In the area of fake news detection, face recognition or SPAM detection, for example, people express greater trust in the decisions made by algorithms than in those made by humans.

So what can be done to maximise AI benefits? I'd like to recommend nine steps going forward:

1. Encourage greater data access for researchers without compromising users' personal privacy.
2. Invest more government funding in unclassified AI research.
3. Promote new models of digital education and AI workforce development so employees have the skills needed in the 21st-century economy.
4. Create a government AI advisory committee to make policy recommendations.
5. Engage with local government and industry governing bodies so they can enact effective policies.
6. Regulate broad AI principles rather than specific algorithms.
7. Take bias complaints seriously so AI does not replicate historic injustice, unfairness, or discrimination in data or algorithms.
8. Maintain mechanisms for human oversight and control.
9. Penalize malicious AI behaviour and promote cybersecurity.

Government moves to regulate and control AI are gaining ground.

China's Cyberspace Administration announced in April 2023, draft regulations for generative AI, the technology behind GPT-4 and domestic rivals like Alibaba's Tongyi Qianwen and Baidu's ERNIE, to ensure the technology adheres to the 'core value of socialism' and does not undermine the government.

The European Union has proposed the 'Artificial Intelligence Act' to govern which kinds of AI are acceptable for use and which should be banned.

US public wariness about AI has yet to translate into federal regulations, but the Biden administration this week announced the launch of public consultations on how to ensure that 'AI systems are legal, effective, ethical, safe, and otherwise trustworthy'.

Summary:

The way AI systems unfold has major implications for society as a whole. It matters how policy issues are addressed, ethical conflicts are reconciled, legal realities are resolved, and how much transparency is required in AI and data analytic solutions. Human choices about software development affect the way in which decisions are made and the way they are integrated into organizational routines. Exactly how these processes are executed needs to be better understood because they will have a substantial impact on the public soon, and for the foreseeable future. AI is already causing a revolution in human affairs and is set to become the single most influential human innovation in history.

'The rise of powerful AI will be either the best or the worst thing ever to happen to humanity. We do not yet know which.' Stephen Hawking, Theoretical physicist (2017)

'What all of us have to do is to make sure we are using AI in a way that is for the benefit of humanity, not to the detriment of humanity.' Tim Cook, CEO of Apple (2017)

Glossary

Machine Learning: A type of AI using algorithms that learn from data to make predictions.

Machine learning typically requires three key ingredients:

- Datasets that provide the examples for training the machine.
- Features that are important components of the data on which the machine is trained to pay attention to and identify patterns.
- Algorithms that are computational rules or steps that govern how the machine should achieve a task. In Deep Learning, these are layered in such a way that the system effectively infers connections.

Artificial Neural Networks: A type of Machine Learning that simulates the computational processes of the brain by recognizing patterns in big sets of structured data.

Deep Learning: A class of Machine Learning that learns without human supervision and involves the layering of many Neural Networks that are designed to recognize patterns in big sets of unstructured data. EG. Image and voice recognition, self-driving cars.

Neural Networks: Algorithms that endeavour to recognize underlying relationships in a set of data through a process that mimics the way the human brain operates. Eg. Credit and loan application evaluation, weather prediction.

Natural Language Processing: A computer program able to understand human language as it is written or spoken. Eg. Speech recognition, text analysis, translation.

Rule-based Expert Systems: A set of logical rules derived from human experts. Eg. Insurance underwriting, credit approval.

Robotic Process Automation: Systems that automate structured digital tasks and interfaces. Eg. Credit card replacement, validating online credentials.

Robots: Automatically operated machines that automate physical activity, manipulate and pick up objects. Eg. Factory and warehouse tasks.

www.ingramcontent.com/pod-product-compliance
Lightning Source LLC
LaVergne TN
LVHW051701050326
832903LV00032B/3938